Designed to Thrive

Designed to Thrive

*Exploring God's Blueprint to Feed
Your Baby with Confidence*

Lindsay Gustafson BSN,
RN, IBCLC

DESIGNED TO THRIVE
Exploring God's Blueprint to Feed Your Baby with Confidence

Copyright © 2025 by Lindsay Gustafson

All Scripture quotations, unless otherwise indicated, are taken from the ESV

Cover design by Abigael Elliott
Editorial Team: Traci Matt, Chloie Benton, Jarah Byron, Kiska Carr
Interior Layout and Design by Alice Briggs

ISBN:
ebook: 979-8-89165-305-4
Paperback: 979-8-89165-306-1
Hardcover: 979-8-89165-307-8

Published by:
Streamline Books
Kansas City, MO
streamlinebookspublishing.com

Contents

Introduction

MY HUSBAND, JOEL, and I had been married just three months when my body started to tell me something was changing. I felt paralyzed by the thought—the swirling unknowns that lay ahead. I was not ready to be a mom. I didn't know how to be a mom. I was only twenty-three years old. I had just married the love of my life and was looking forward to starting the life we had dreamt about during our engagement. Everything seemed to come to an alarming halt as the tides of change swelled as big as my emotions and tears that didn't seem to stop. Bringing a child into the world felt so intimidating, and I was full of fear—fear that I wouldn't be a good mom and that I would fail. I didn't have time to plan or get used to the idea of starting a family; it was happening now.

I remember something profound my father-in-law, Tim, told Joel and me as we sat in his office, afraid of these sudden changes and seeking some sort of solace and reassurance. Tim is a pastor and an incredible counselor. He simply said, "The Lord gives life" (Gen. 2:7) with the warmest smile. This short and sweet statement shook the fear out of me almost immediately. I felt an indescribable and undeniable peace in that very moment. He wasn't upset, mad, or angry at us. He wasn't worried about our future, and he did not tell us that we wouldn't be able to do it. He was full of grace and encouragement. He helped me feel adequate and confident that I was going to be a great mom and that we would be great parents. Tim went on to explain how the Lord had chosen this time specifically for me to carry this baby and for Joel and me to become parents. The Lord does not make mistakes. We prayed together, we wept, and we proceeded forth in faith, trust, and hope for the future. We walked in full surrender and confidence that the Lord would sustain us and provide for our every need.

After that encounter and conversation, my perspective shifted, and I began to move through my pregnancy with confidence. The Lord was with me, and He was never leaving me (Joshua 1:9). Now, don't get me wrong—the pregnancy was not all sunshine and rainbows, that's for sure! I struggled with massive morning sickness, fatigue, and continued self-doubt. I had to cry out to God for strength of body and mind as I journeyed closer to meeting this sweet baby earthside. I remember lying in bed praying and listening to the song "Sweep Me Away" on repeat as I battled constant nausea and fatigue. I prepared the best I knew how, but there were so many things I did not have the understanding or frame of reference for. You see, I simply didn't know what I didn't know. It was 2006, way before any social media platforms we have today were available. Today, social media allows us access to information on pretty much everything, immediately, anytime, anyplace. This was both a blessing and a hardship as I look back on my experience of becoming a new mom.

New Beginnings

The sunlight warmed the room with a greenhouse effect through the large windows that overlooked rows of cars in the parking lot below. It was a perfect spring day—the perfect day to have a baby. My husband and my sister-in-law coached me and fed me ice chips. I was leaning over the side of the bed, swaying and humming through a contraction when suddenly my phone began to ring. It was Josh, the admissions counselor for Saint Luke's Nursing School in Kansas City, Missouri. I did not answer, but I received a voicemail with the amazing news that I had been accepted into nursing school for the fall class of 2007. My dream of becoming a nurse was coming to fruition.

I didn't have much time to process the news as contractions continued, wave after wave. I was getting so close to meeting my first baby girl. As a first-time mom, I had absolutely no idea what to expect with labor, birth, breastfeeding, and motherhood. I was too young and naive to realize it could be hard. I was expectant and full of joy and awe.

My labor started slow but quickly progressed after I received an epidural at five centimeters dilated. One hour after my epidural placement, I was resting on my side when I distinctly remember the nurses bursting through the door to check on me and the baby—her heart rate was dropping. My doctor rushed in the room to place internal monitors to track the baby's heart rate and measure the strength of the contractions more accurately. As she went to insert them, she exclaimed, "Oh! We won't be needing these—you're ten centimeters, and the baby is coming now!"

The baby had descended so quickly, and I had dilated so rapidly, that her heart rate was decelerating. The team quickly prepared the room, and just a few pushes later, our girl arrived and was placed in my arms. I was in complete shock. I tried to focus on her sweet face and tiny features, but I was not feeling well. I had lost a significant amount of blood during delivery and needed extra medication to get it under control. I felt very weak, exhausted, and nauseous for most of the evening, and I had a hard time focusing on Lily and breastfeeding. The nurses were amazing, helping me to ensure she latched well, since I couldn't get her latched myself. The rest of my hospital stay was a whirlwind, leaving little time to comprehend that I was now a mother, responsible for another tiny human.

Panic set in when we arrived home to our first apartment as a family of three. In that moment, I was struck with the realization that we were completely responsible for making sure she was nourished and cared for. We were trusted to keep her alive and to raise her well. I felt utterly unprepared and full of fear. Everything felt like it was crashing down. I had no idea how to be a mom, and I could not get her to stop crying. I did not know how to calm and soothe her, how to feed her, or how to help her fall asleep. I was in pain, exhausted, and completely wrecked with the changes my body had endured. The adrenaline and excitement from birth had worn off, all the visitors were gone, and it was just us left to figure out how to be good parents. Lily and I cried together as I held her close. My husband did his best to console and encourage me, but I could tell he was terrified too. Through streaming tears, I looked up and prayed to God that He would help me learn to be a good mom and raise my daughter well. I prayed He would stand in the gap, protect her, and redeem the situations where I would fall short.

With the help of our family and small group at church, we figured it out. Lily was such a sweet baby and showed me so much grace (her middle name) as I learned to be a mom. We went on walks every day, and she was my best errand-running girl. I was so nervous to start nursing school and have to be away from her. We were just beginning to find our rhythm when it was time for me to start classes. She was four months old, and my incredible mother-in-law, Renee, was so kind and selfless to watch her for me while I attended class. I knew Lily was in the best hands while I had to be away from her, which was so comforting.

The beginning of the end of our breastfeeding relationship started here. To this day, it saddens me that I was forced to wean before either of us were ready. Breastfeeding had come easily for Lily and me after a night nurse at the hospital showed me how to latch her at 3:00 a.m. that first night she was born. From that moment on, we never looked back. I was able to latch her well on my own after that successful feeding. She breastfed exclusively for four months without difficulty—until I started nursing school.

Everything changed due to my lack of education and understanding about milk supply and demand. I had milk stored in the freezer that I had pumped before starting school, so she had bottles to drink while I was in class. I was never taught and didn't realize that I needed to be pumping while I was away from her. After two weeks without pumping, my milk supply significantly decreased, and she could no longer get enough milk from directly nursing. I did not know what to do, so I started giving her formula bottles after nursing. That was the point of no return. Once I started to give formula bottles, I started producing less and less milk until she wouldn't latch or nurse at all. I had absolutely no idea what happened at the time. I thought my milk just "dried up out of nowhere." I simply didn't know what I didn't know. Looking back on my experience, I know now that there were multiple factors that played a role in my early weaning. First, I had a used breast pump; second, I had incorrect flange sizing; and third, I was not pumping to maintain my supply when I was away from my baby.

I can say with confidence that taking a prenatal breastfeeding class and scheduling a back-to-school or work consult would have benefitted me so much and would have protected my ability to breastfeed Lily longer. I did not have any knowledge or understanding about how my body produced milk, how to properly use a breast pump, or how to ensure breastfeeding and milk supply were maintained. I also didn't even know lactation consultants existed. I believe if I had known this and met with a lactation consultant right away, I would have been able to ramp up my milk supply and get back into a new rhythm with breastfeeding, pumping, and bottle feeding.

I wish I had the help back then, and it is part of what drove me into this profession. I want all moms to have access to quality education and support to help them reach their goals, so they do not have to wean before they are ready. Growing in knowledge and understanding helps create confidence, and access to ongoing support and encouragement is vital in helping moms succeed.

My goals in writing this book are to provide you with clinical expertise and uplifting support, to help you trust your innate intuition, and to lead you to cultivate the confidence you need for you and your baby to thrive together and flourish in this precious life. I will guide you through the process of lactation and breastfeeding step by step—beginning with the biological and physiologic design of breastfeeding. I will also discuss common challenges and teach you how to troubleshoot and manage them effectively, along with knowing when to seek professional, hands-on support.

With the understanding and insight gained from this book, my hope is for you to grow in confidence and become able to relax and enjoy your time with your sweet babe. I will teach you the skills necessary to understand newborn biological feeding norms and how to determine quality feeding for your baby, so you can enjoy your newborn without these common added stressors. When babies are feeding well, they are sleeping well, digestion is working well, and they are content little squishes. When babies are thriving, moms are thriving. Moms are happy, calm, confident, full of peace—soaking up all the precious newborn snuggles.

The Calling

As each has received a gift, use it to serve one another, as
good stewards of God's varied grace: whoever speaks, as
one who speaks oracles of God; whoever serves, as one who
serves by the strength that God supplies—in order that in
everything God may be glorified through Jesus Christ. To
Him belong glory and dominion forever and ever. Amen.
1 Peter 4:10-11

I WAS RUNNING OUT of hope. I found myself at the end of my very long and challenging labor with my second baby. I labored all night in and out of the tub, with my faithful and amazing husband and doula by my side. They took turns encouraging me and supporting me through each uterine surge. I remember saying multiple times to Heather, my incredible doula, "I can't do this," and she would promptly respond, her voice steady and confident, "But you are doing it." Each surge was a step forward, progress in bringing my sweet daughter closer and closer to being in my arms. The dark of night was relentless and seemed never-ending as contraction after contraction continued.

1

I remember thinking to myself at that time, *The night is darkest just before dawn.* I could hear my husband's soothing voice saying, "His mercies are new every morning." I knew I just had to make it until morning, and I would be okay. I could do it.

The sun finally started to rise, and shift change was happening. I remember the fresh new labor nurse's purple scrubs and curly brown hair as she entered the room full of confidence and compassion. She was amazing. She immediately brought the wind back to my sails with her presence. She knew just what to do, and my baby calmly made her entrance with the most beautiful birth on a bright, cheerful early July morning. My inspiring nurse, Sarah Darby, honored all my wishes and hopes for my birth experience. She fiercely protected me, advocated for my baby, and was so calm and trusting in my body and my baby as sweet Adelyn Eden entered the world. I am forever grateful for her and the experience she helped me to accomplish. She was so empowering.

She is the reason I began to feel and hear my calling from God to be a labor nurse just like her. I wanted other mamas to experience what I experienced with her caring for me and my baby. She impacted me for life, and I will never forget her. When I thanked her, she replied with, "I only brought out what was already inside you. Sometimes women need women to remind us of our strength." I found out after the fact that she was studying to become a midwife, and what an incredible midwife she is to this day—empowering and supporting women as she did for me fifteen years ago. I prayed that the right doors would open for me to become a labor and delivery nurse after I graduated nursing school just ten months after Adelyn was born, and they did.

I had done lots of reading, researching, and preparing in anticipation of an unmedicated, natural childbirth with Adelyn. My labor and birth with Lily had been difficult, and I did not like the feeling of being out of control in my body with an epidural. I was so sick afterward from losing all the extra blood that it made it hard for me to remember the *golden hour*—those first sixty minutes with Lily. I could barely remember holding her after she was born.

It was a bit of a traumatic experience, and I knew after that I needed to educate myself prior to my second birth. I read about physiological childbirth and gained understanding on the stages of labor, how the amazing female body progresses through labor to birth, and how incredible the bonding and overall experience can be. I read about how without medical intervention recovery times are shorter and easier, babies breastfeed better, babies are more alert, and stress hormones are lower after birth.

When women know the natural birthing process, that knowledge and education create confidence and thus lower stress levels. Lower stress levels yield peace and relaxation, help oxytocin (also known as the *cuddle* or *love hormone*) to flow more freely, and encourage bonding and nurture to begin. Holding your baby skin-to-skin right at birth stabilizes baby's vital signs and syncs up mom and baby to be able to co-regulate together. The co-regulation helps with bonding and breastfeeding and an overall feeling of safety, security, and connectedness.

Each type of birth can have its own unique set of challenges that can impact breastfeeding. Cesarean sections can impact mom and baby's alertness, making it difficult to latch initially. Mom's mobility is limited due to anesthesia and pain, which makes it difficult to position and latch well. Research shows that milk supply can be delayed because the normal cascade of hormones with physiologic birth does not happen with a surgical birth. I experienced a C-section with my fourth baby, and I can say breastfeeding was more challenging than with my unmedicated vaginal births. I think I would have struggled a lot more without having my previous knowledge and understanding from breastfeeding my other babies.

Vaginal deliveries can also have complications that can interfere with breastfeeding. Sometimes labor is long, and the pushing stage is hard and stressful for both mom and baby. The birth can be traumatic, or there can be excess bleeding that leaves mom exhausted and can impact how quickly milk supply transitions in. Medicated vaginal births can also affect mom and baby in the initial breastfeeding initiation. Whether it is from an epidural or intravenous (IV) pain medication, baby's alertness and eagerness to nurse are dampened. During an induction of labor with Pitocin (the synthetic form of oxytocin used to induce contractions), the typical hormone response in the body has interference and endorphins are not released the same way. Sometimes, this can impact initial bonding and the natural drop in stress hormones after birth.

Home birth also poses some challenges that can arise with initiating breastfeeding. Usually, babies can tap into all their innate wiring and reflexes to help them latch and nurse well because there was no intervention with the natural physiologic birthing process and no medications on board. The challenge can be a lack of understanding and education surrounding breastfeeding, especially with first-time moms. After the midwife and doula leave, mom and baby are without the support of hospital nursing and lactation staff.

I experienced many of these challenges. My first birth was medicated with both epidural and IV pain medicine and was also complicated by postpartum hemorrhage. I did not feel well, and I was in a daze for the first several hours, making it difficult to hold my baby skin-to-skin, bond, and initiate breastfeeding. My nurses were amazing and helped make sure my baby was latching and doing well while I was unable to do it myself. My second and third births were both completely unmedicated hospital births with zero intervention, and they were by far my easiest for initiating breastfeeding. My fourth birth was spontaneous labor that turned into a C-section. The most challenging thing about that experience was managing my own pain and limited mobility while fighting through the sadness, feelings of failure, and emotional battle of having an unexpected outcome with needing a surgical birth.

As you can see, challenges and difficulties can arise regardless of how your birth unfolds. I feel it is important to be aware of potential obstacles that may complicate the process and to know that help and guidance are available if needed. With knowledge, realistic expectations, and excellent support, challenges can be mitigated, allowing for successful bonding, nurturing, and breastfeeding.

The initiation of breastfeeding is highly important not only for baby's health and well-being but also for mom's establishment of milk supply and the emotional connection and bond that develops between them. While medical circumstances may sometimes necessitate interruptions or deviations from a birth plan, understanding the next steps is essential. For example, if baby needs to go for observation to the neonatal intensive care unit (NICU) after birth, how does the plan shift to ensure the breastfeeding relationship is protected?

A lactation consultant full of compassionate care and excellent clinical knowledge can help guide and direct you. Emotional support and clinical support are both equally important. When you have the support of a lactation consultant that understands this balance—offering encouragement while simultaneously helping with the clinical side of everything—this can be the catalyst to carry you to your goals when you are feeling discouraged, overwhelmed, and not sure where to start.

Expect the Unexpected

Megan, a client of mine, was thirty-four weeks pregnant when I met with her to go over breastfeeding education and help her feel prepared for birth. She was eager to learn and ready to become a mom. Her excitement and anticipation absolutely radiated. A couple of days later, she called me crying and upset after receiving the news that her labor needed to be induced due to high blood pressure. She was terrified that breastfeeding was not going to work out, and she was sad knowing that the birth she had planned and dreamt about would not happen. I reassured her, comforted her, and uplifted her, letting her know I was there for her every step of the way. We talked through how the labor and birth process might look different with an induction and a preterm baby. I helped her set realistic expectations for breastfeeding and explained how to ensure milk supply would be stimulated and established well. We also discussed how she could accomplish bonding when her baby needed to go to the NICU shortly after birth. Having a clearer picture of the process and tangible strategies helped put her mind at ease while processing, preparing, and feeling encouraged that she could do it.

Megan went in for her induction, and her beautiful baby was born without difficulties. Sweet baby Amelia was admitted to the NICU shortly after birth for respiratory support but was stable and doing well. Megan was able to kiss her baby and snuggle her cheek before the NICU team transported Amelia to her room. Within an hour after birth, Megan began hand expression and pumping. Her husband captured pictures and videos of Amelia for Megan to watch while pumping to help increase her oxytocin to yield more milk output. She also was given a special lovey that she could tuck into her hospital gown to absorb her scent that could be taken and put in Amelia's crib. She was able to make it to Amelia's room after her recovery period was completed, and she was able to hold Amelia skin-to-skin for the first time when Amelia was a little over two hours old. Megan pumped every two to three hours around the clock and held Amelia skin-to-skin as often as she could. Her milk transitioned fully around day four postpartum, and she was able to collect substantial milk volumes with the pump. She continued pumping and providing her milk for Amelia until Amelia was stable enough to begin working on latching directly to the breast.

With time and patience, Amelia was able to latch and exclusively breastfeed. Getting NICU babies to the point where they can exclusively breastfeed and take full feedings is a process, but Megan was dedicated and determined. She did it. We communicated a lot during her hospital stay, and I visited the NICU often to help her with latching, pumping, and understanding the expectations for premature babies' growth and development and how it impacts breastfeeding. Megan and Amelia went on to nurse for eighteen months. I love Megan's story because it shows how unexpected circumstances can still lead to successful outcomes. It encourages moms that though there can be all kinds of different challenges or difficulties, we can still work toward and find success.

Stepping Out in Faith

I was chosen for an internship, or capstone course, at the end of my senior year of nursing school to work nights on a labor and delivery (L&D) floor, and I was ecstatic. My passion and calling were falling into place and coming to fruition. L&D was highly competitive, and securing a position immediately after nursing school graduation without prior experience was challenging. The Lord smiled on me and prepared the way. I began to walk through the doors He opened for me to live my purpose. I worked at that hospital as an L&D nurse for thirteen years. I learned and grew so much as a nurse, a person, and a mom. I am forever grateful for the experience I had there.

I began my coursework and journey to becoming an International Board Certified Lactation Consultant (IBCLC) when my fourth baby was about three months old. The IBCLC credential is the gold standard in lactation care. I was working weekend night shifts (Friday and Saturday nights from 7:00 p.m. to 7:00 a.m.) at the hospital and taking lactation courses online during the day. I was blown away by the depth of knowledge required to fully understand lactation, including how it works and how to problem-solve to help moms succeed in reaching their goals. Lactation consulting is much more than simply helping babies latch—it goes so much deeper. The depth is part of what makes me love this work so much, though. I love to assess, problem-solve, and create care plans that lead to success.

Another aspect of my job that I deeply cherish is providing emotional support and encouragement to the moms and families I serve. To earn the IBCLC credential, I completed ninety-five hours of lactation-specific education, a thousand clinical hours of offering breastfeeding support, fourteen hours of health science classes, five hours of communication classes; and I passed an international board exam. After I earned my IBCLC license, I worked full-time in the hospital's lactation department for a year and a half before transitioning to private practice. I learned so much supporting breastfeeding mamas immediately after birth in the L&D unit, during their stay on the mother/baby unit, and while supporting moms and babies in the NICU. I felt a pull and a longing to step out into private practice because I wanted to provide the continuity of care and long-term support for breastfeeding mamas for the duration of their journey. In the hospital, time constraints often prevented me from offering the level of holistic and thorough support that mothers and babies needed.

The best decision I ever made was to step out in faith and run after something I am so passionate about and feel is absolutely my calling. I am exactly where God wants me. Every day, I am humbled by the job I get to do that does not feel like work at all. Words cannot describe how fulfilled and honored I am to care for moms and babies in this way.

Look for Holistic Care

Have you ever had that feeling where you just click with someone you've encountered? You can feel it in your bones, and you might even get goosebumps as you realize just how tightly you align. You relax and exhale your worry as you feel connected and immediately supported; you feel seen. This, to me, is the jewel on top of the gold that sets apart different providers. So how do you find that person in the sea of professional support?

There are two critical components to being an effective lactation consultant. First, you have to hold impeccable clinical skill and knowledge—this includes holistic and thorough assessment skills. Second, you have to offer validating emotional support and truly "see" the mom and baby sitting in front of you. You have to be able to deliver sensitive information in a way that is uplifting and encouraging, rather than hopeless and intimidating.

As a holistic lactation consultant, I assess the body as a unit when determining the root cause of the difficulties, pain, or challenges. My background in nursing, lactation, and Craniosacral Fascial Therapy (CFT) allows me to approach care comprehensively rather than focusing solely on the baby's mouth or the mother's breast anatomy. CFT is a gentle treatment modality that combines myofascial release and craniosacral therapy to help relax fascial strain throughout the body. Fascia, the connective tissue between muscle and skin, can tighten and impact mobility and comfort. Since the fascial web connects from the tongue to the toes, tension or tightness in one area of the body can impact others.

I sought CFT training to help me understand the link between body tension and feeding difficulties. This understanding completely changed my practice. I was able to see results immediately while releasing fascial tension and strain to help babies be able to position, latch, and feed comfortably and efficiently. The knowledge I have in oral motor function, lactation, breastfeeding, newborn reflexes, and the fascial system helps me to be able to intervene on a deeper level. It's important to find root causes so moms and babies find comfort and success and truly enjoy feeding times. I am grateful to have learned this gentle treatment modality to compliment my work as a registered nurse and lactation consultant.

Natasha was a client of mine who called me as a last-ditch effort to get her baby to latch and breastfeed. Her baby had never been able to latch from birth, and her pediatrician told her that her baby was "not built to breastfeed." It broke my heart listening to her story. Her baby, Ruben, was four weeks old when she called me to schedule a consult. She had been pumping around the clock to maintain her milk supply, and although Ruben was drinking bottles well, she longed to latch him at the breast and nurse him. She was not able to get him to latch.

During our first visit, I could not get Ruben to latch either. After my assessment, I explained to her that the difficulty was not because of his mouth or her anatomy but rather his overall body tension. He was in flexion and did not have the mobility to get into a comfortable position to latch at all. We began oral exercises, facial massage, among other specific techniques, including CFT, to help release his tension so his body could relax, allowing him to achieve optimal positioning and latching. After three CFT treatments, Ruben was latching and breastfeeding exclusively. Natasha worked tirelessly on pumping, maintaining her milk supply, and gently encouraging Ruben through his exercises and latching attempts. They made progress day by day. She persevered through an emotional journey, but she succeeded.

This is just one example of how a thorough holistic assessment, compassionate care with emotional support, and unique treatment and care plans can lead to success and the fulfillment of goals. The mother and baby went on to breastfeed exclusively for over a year.

Many times, I see new moms who are desperate for answers. They want their babies to be happy, comfortable, and well-fed. They end up receiving mixed and conflicting messages from so many different people and providers that they become completely overwhelmed and have no idea where to start. They begin to lose hope that they can resolve the issues causing their baby's discomfort. This is where lactation support comes in! There is hope and there is help.

Below are common issues lactation consultants help with:

- Prenatal breastfeeding education
- Painful/difficult latching
- Establishing and maintaining milk supply
- Breastfeeding preterm, late preterm, and early term babies
- Breastfeeding multiples
- Tandem nursing
- Babies with slow weight gain
- Assessment, care plan, and oral habilitation for tongue-tied babies
- Low milk supply/oversupply
- Mastitis and plugged ducts
- Breast pump education and flange fitting
- Bottle-feeding
- Returning to work strategies for maintaining milk supply and protecting the breastfeeding relationship
- Babies' gas, spit up, reflux, or discomfort during or after feedings
- Strategies for combo feeding
- Starting solid foods with baby
- Strategies for weaning

There are many reasons new parents schedule lactation consultations. Sometimes it is due to difficulty or pain with latching, and we walk through optimal positioning and latching techniques to ensure a proper latch and effective milk transfer. I also conduct a full assessment of both mom and baby to determine the root cause nipple pain or trauma, working toward healing and correcting the problem.

Other times, concerns may include low milk supply, poor weight gain, excessive gas, frequent spitting up, or overall discomfort. Being a lactation consultant is a lot like detective work. When meeting a new client, I assess the situation holistically, considering all variables that could be contributing to the symptoms. I then create a plan for forward progress.

I often see babies whom parents describe as uncomfortable when lying on their backs, grunting, and squirming as if they cannot relax into a restful sleep. Often, this discomfort stems from suboptimal feeding quality, leading to digestive symptoms. The peristalsis of the gastrointestinal (GI) tract begins with the tongue. Peristalsis starts with the wavelike motion the tongue makes during swallowing, helping to protect the airway as liquid or food is ingested. Peristalsis continues in the GI tract as part of the digestive process, including absorption and elimination. If the mouth is tight and the neck is flexed, tongue movement is limited or dysfunctional, impacting digestion, milk transfer, and regulation of milk flow. This can lead to GI discomfort, including gas, spit-up, and difficulty with bowel movements.

Additionally, oral dysfunction may stem from tension. Part of my assessment includes determining whether body tension is causing oral dysfunction or if the oral dysfunction is causing tension. This cycle must be addressed at its root for progress to be made. Digestion is also greatly impacted by tension.

My true desire is to help you and your baby thrive and flourish by offering clinical expertise, compassionate care, and uplifting support. I feel honored and humbled to be entrusted with supporting families during such a vulnerable time. There is no doubt in my mind that God prepared me for this career through my experiences as a labor and delivery nurse and becoming a mom myself. My entire career has been in women's and children's health, and I am blessed to be walking in this specific calling the Lord has placed on my life.

The Biological Design

For you formed my inward parts; you knitted
me together in my mother's womb.
Psalm 139:13

T HIS SECTION FOCUSES on prenatal education and
understanding the process our bodies go through when we
lactate and produce milk (lactogenesis). I will also discuss
two of the most important components of breastfeeding that work
synergistically: nourish and nurture. Having a solid understanding
of how the breastfeeding process was biologically and physiologically
designed greatly impacts your ability to succeed and meet your goals
of breastfeeding your baby.

Nourish

Just how do our bodies make milk for our babies to thrive? There
are four stages of lactogenesis that our bodies go through during
pregnancy, birth, and postpartum.

Stage 1 begins around week sixteen of pregnancy. This is when our body begins to produce colostrum, our very first milk. Initially, this process is completely hormonally controlled. Some women may begin leaking colostrum during pregnancy, while others may not. This is not indicative of how much milk you will make when your baby arrives. The hormonal shifts during pregnancy prepare the breasts for making milk. You might notice an increase in size, sensitivity, darker or larger areolar tissue, and increased veining. As your body is changing and going through different stages during pregnancy, your body is also preparing to nourish your baby after birth.

Stage 2 begins after birth when the placenta is delivered. God designed our bodies and created this process with intricate perfection. After the placenta is delivered, we get a major shift in hormones—a sharp drop in progesterone and a rise in prolactin—that tells our bodies the baby is here and it's now time to begin the next phase of making mature milk, now that the placenta is no longer providing nutrients. Babies typically begin latching and drinking colostrum within the first one to two hours after the birth.

Let's talk about colostrum. You might have heard it referenced as *liquid gold*, which is a very fitting name. This first milk is produced in small amounts and is thick, packing a powerful punch of essential nutrients. It is designed perfectly for easy digestion, has a very specific composition, is full of antibodies to protect baby, is designed with a natural laxative component to help babies pass meconium (their first, thick, tarry stools), among many other benefits.[1] Babies will typically drink about 2-10 milliliters of colostrum per feeding during the first twenty-four hours, which is only ½ to 2 teaspoons total per feeding— very small amounts! But why such small volumes? Several reasons.

First, babies' tummies are small—about the size of a cherry at birth. This means they need to feed frequently, which also provides the adequate stimulation a mother needs to help her body establish her milk supply. Milk establishment transitions from an endocrine control to autocrine control as hormones shift after birth and the maternal body is stimulated to produce more milk. You can begin to see the biological design as it was intended, the intricate maternal-baby connection.[2]

Second, we also need to remember that baby has just filled their lungs with air for the first time. Baby is transitioning to survive life without the support of the placenta in multiple ways. Baby now has to latch and coordinate sucking, swallowing, and breathing all at the same time. If mothers began with large amounts of breast milk initially, it would overwhelm the baby. They would be flooded with milk and choke. Colostrum is thick and is transferred from the breast in just drops at a time, allowing baby to manage the liquid and maintain a rhythmic suck/swallow pattern that helps soothe, nurture, and nourish them.

Third, when a baby is nursing or bottle feeding, they are receiving input at the roof of their mouth—stimulating the vagus nerve, which is responsible for the rest and digest function of the nervous system. This allows baby to feel the calming effect, nourishment from the colostrum, as well as soothing from the act of suckling. If feeding difficulties are present, babies will not have the same calming, soothing, and enjoyment effect that feeding should afford them. This can cause a cycle of discomfort and difficulty to continue. New moms and parents can start to feel helpless and hopeless when challenges persist, and babies are impacted. Feeding difficulties lead to digestion difficulties, which lead to discomfort and fussiness.

Frequent latching and stimulation to the breast after the baby is born is essential, as it helps to grow the milk-making cells to be able to support the increased milk volume that is going to transition in the next few days. Transitional and mature milk will arrive more quickly and with more volume as baby latches well and frequently in the first few days. If adequate stimulation does not occur in the first few days postpartum, overall milk supply may be impacted greatly.

Mature milk usually starts to appear between days three and five postpartum. As this shift occurs, it is crucial to ensure that milk is removed regularly from the breasts (every two to three hours). Ideally, the baby would be nursing on demand, signaling the mom's body to regulate the volume of milk the baby needs. If complications arise with mom or baby that limit the ability to directly breastfeed, or if exclusive pumping is desired, it is important to remove milk from the breast via breast pump every three hours to maintain an adequate milk supply. By four weeks postpartum, the transition to mature milk is usually complete. Breast milk composition will continue to change as the baby grows, meeting nutritional needs.

Understanding the process of establishing milk supply is essential from the very beginning. Most cases of low milk supply I encounter are due to misunderstandings or mismanagement of breastfeeding and milk removal in the first two weeks.

Stage 3 occurs when milk supply is fully regulated by supply and demand. Lactation shifts from being hormonally controlled to autocrine control. This is important to understand because if our bodies did not go through this change, we could not wean and stop making milk. Continued lactation depends on the removal of milk from the breast to tell our brains to keep making milk. Milk production depends on the regular removal of milk; if milk is not removed, the body signals that less milk is needed, causing supply to decrease.

If you remember back to when I discussed the decrease in milk supply that happened to me when I started nursing school during my breastfeeding journey with Lily, this is why I ran into that difficulty. I did not understand supply and demand, and that my body would start making less milk if I stopped removing the milk frequently when I was away from her.

This brings us to **Stage 4**, or the weaning stage. During this stage, our breasts return to their pre-pregnant state. The complete involution can take up to forty days.

The weaning process is different for everyone. Some women decide they are ready to wean, while others may be forced to do so due to medical reasons or medications. Regardless of the situation, it can be beneficial to meet with a lactation consultant to discuss weaning strategies and avoid complications such as plugged ducts and mastitis. Support through this process helps prevent stress and fosters confidence, while having someone along for the journey.

Nourishment from breastfeeding is extremely important and beneficial for the baby's development. Breast milk is perfectly designed to support immunity, gut microbiome, brain development, and growth, as well as to protect against childhood illnesses like respiratory infections, gastrointestinal infections, and even childhood cancers. The composition is intricate, and the amounts of the different components change monthly, daily, and even hourly to match what the baby needs.

Breast milk has protective antibodies that are particularly remarkable. If the mother is exposed to an illness, her body immediately begins producing specific antibodies to that illness, which are transferred through the milk to protect the baby. Likewise, when the baby is exposed to something, the saliva exchange at the nipple triggers the mother's body to create antibodies for that illness. This phenomenon is part of God's design, as it also helps babies avoid allergies by exposing them to allergens through breast milk.

The same effect happens when a mom kisses baby's face and head. I believe this is one of the reasons why moms are obsessed with, and intoxicated by, their baby's smell and touch. They are drawn to kiss them all the time. Breast milk can also protect babies against food allergies as they are exposed to allergens through the breast milk. It is essential that babies are consuming breast milk at adequate volumes to grow and develop into robust and healthy babies. The foundation of nutrients and antibodies will serve them as they grow throughout childhood and into adulthood.

Here is a list of key components of breast milk:

1. Oligosaccharides (prebiotics) help colonize the baby's gut with good bacteria to protect against infections entering the bloodstream.
2. Immunoglobulins or antibodies help protect the baby against viruses and illness.
3. Growth factors help to support healthy development.
4. Live cells, which include white blood cells and stem cells, help organs to develop and heal.
5. Proteins and amino acids help baby grow and develop, activate their immune system, and develop and protect neurons in the brain.
6. Enzymes aid in digestion, immune system function, and iron absorption.
7. Long-chain fatty acids help build the nervous system and aid in brain and eye development.
8. Hormones help to regulate baby's appetite, sleep, and bonding.
9. Vitamins and minerals support healthy growth and development and help baby to develop healthy teeth and bones.
10. MicroRNAs help to prevent or halt disease development, support baby's immune system, and regulate gene expression.
11. Fat, protein, and carbohydrates provide essential nutrition.[3]

Nurture

Although highly important, it's easy to get hyper-fixated on the nourishing component of breastfeeding—worrying about how much baby is drinking, and if they are getting enough milk. We sometimes completely forget about the second highly critical component of breastfeeding: nurture. Breastfeeding was designed with the purpose to both nourish and nurture our baby. This is why I find teaching the biologic and physiologic design of breastfeeding critical in helping new moms have realistic expectations for breastfeeding. It's important to take both into account when determining how baby is doing. Their feeding patterns should be following biological norms for their age. I love teaching how to assess feeding quality and the outward signs to look for when determining if baby is drinking appropriate volumes for growth and health.

It is impossible to see how much milk babies drink at the breast. This can cause stress and anxiety when parents are unaware of the signs that provide confidence in feeding. Some reassuring indicators include recognizing an active sucking pattern with audible or visible swallowing, relaxation of the baby's body during feeding, contentment after feeding, and adequate diaper output.

Nurture, bonding, and secure attachment are essential to healthy infant growth and development. One of the primary challenges I observe in my practice that can interfere with bonding in the postpartum period is feeding difficulties. These difficulties can cause high levels of stress for new parents. Stress hormones can impact many aspects for new moms including physical and emotional postpartum healing, milk supply, confidence, and sleep. This applies to both breastfeeding and bottle-feeding breast milk or formula. Understanding what quality feeding looks like—both at breast and from the bottle—and how to achieve optimal feeding is of utmost importance when ensuring that babies thrive and that new moms flourish in their new roles. When hiccups or unexpected challenges arise, they can lead to several consequences: a mom losing confidence in her ability to feed her baby well, stress from uncertainty, doubt in her innate intuition, and ultimately, an impact on her overall joy.

Do you remember when it first hit you—the undeniable bonding moment with your baby? Was it when you felt that warm gel drop onto your tummy for the first time and saw a tiny flutter, flickering too quickly to count? Maybe it was when your phone rang in the middle of the night and you received the news that the brave mama carrying your soon to be baby was in labor, or when you were handed your precious baby to hold for the first time. Maybe it was when you received the call informing you that you had been selected to adopt a baby by a courageous birth mother. This special bond can begin at any moment and looks different for everyone. One thing I know to be true: The bond between mother and baby is unlike any other on earth. It is unique and only strengthens as you get to know each other and begin life connected—synced in intricate rhythms.

I believe it is a sweet gift from God to be able to feel our babies move from the inside. It seems He designed pregnancy this way to help us begin bonding with our babies long before they join us outside the womb. It is a gentle, sweet reminder that we are carrying, protecting, and nurturing precious cargo within us. It all feels miraculous. When you stop to reflect on conception, embryonic and fetal development, labor, birth, and breastfeeding, God's handiwork is undeniable. I believe bonding can begin even while baby is still in the womb.

Becoming a mother forever changes you. Did you know there is evidence of fetal cells from each pregnancy a woman has that are found in the maternal brain even years later?[4] I believe God specifically designed it this way for a purpose.

A Special Note to Adoptive Parents

I want to take a moment to write a note here to the adoptive mamas: You are incredible; you are brave. Your situation may be unique, but God has chosen you to be your baby's mom. God is good; you will also bond to your baby, even if your baby did not grow in your womb. When He created your baby, He also chose you. It's your story that

He wrote, before you were even born. To the biological mamas that have chosen adoption for their babies, God sees you and loves you and your sweet baby. You have chosen life for your baby—this is sacrificial love, the type of love that parallels Jesus' love for each of us. You are incredible and strong, and your baby is loved. We are all adopted, in a way, into God's family. To those who have been adopted themselves, you were created by God with a specific purpose and your story is beautiful and perfect and utterly amazing. You are chosen and you are loved and cherished beyond measure.

Adoptive parents, you can bond with your baby. What an incredible gift you are. I am so grateful for you. You have chosen to love and cherish and raise up a child and give them amazing earthly parents. You were also chosen to be the parents for this precious, sweet gift. You were hand-chosen and you are perfect. It might feel overwhelming and scary, and you might question if you will form a strong bond with a child that you did not carry in your womb. I'm going to tell you that you can. I have worked with many adoptive parents to help teach and guide them in newborn care and infant feeding. I teach the same principles that I teach biological parents on the innate design and needs of the infant, and how we are created as humans in the image of God to bond, love, grow, nurture, and be nurtured.

I have worked with families that learned important feeding skills and gained knowledge and understanding prior to babe's arrival so they felt confident heading into the life transition of bringing a newborn baby home. Feeling confident, having tools, and most importantly, having unwavering support in your corner are all key to providing the best start for your new family member. The ongoing support will help you feel unafraid and unashamed, and it will help cultivate the confidence you need. From day one, you will truly enjoy this beautiful time with your sweet baby as your family grows.

God's Incredible Blueprint

Throughout this book, I will answer some important questions I hear often from moms I am supporting:

- How do I latch and feed my baby?
- How do I know if my baby is getting enough milk and is doing well?
- How can I bond with my baby and ensure they feel nurtured?

Understanding the biological feeding norms and setting realistic expectations are two key pieces to the puzzle. Newborn babies are reflexive feeders for the first several weeks. They rely on their innate reflexes to help them survive and get nourishment as they learn. Babies depend on their moms, dads, and caregivers to help them feel safe and secure while feeding, and to trigger the reflexes necessary for a good latch and effective feeding.

Think about your own experience eating and drinking. If you are stressed or your environment does not feel safe and secure, it becomes difficult to relax, making eating a stressful experience. You might eat too quickly or not want to eat at all. When your nervous system is in a fight-or-flight response, it is hard to focus on nourishment. Babies cannot trigger their suck reflex and be in fight-or-flight simultaneously. Stressful feeding situations also impact moms during breastfeeding. Oxytocin is responsible for the milk ejection reflex. If a baby is upset, crying, and struggling to latch, the mom's stress level may rise as well, making it difficult for her milk to let down and flow easily. The release of oxytocin is inhibited by stress and/or pain.[5]

Letdown, also known as the milk ejection reflex, occurs when oxytocin, the hormone released from the mother's anterior pituitary gland, triggers the reflex. This causes milk to be pushed out of the alveoli, where it is stored, through smooth muscle contraction, into the milk ducts, and out through the nipple pores. Oxytocin is released through nipple stimulation, breast massage, hearing a baby cry, looking at pictures or videos of your baby, among other triggers.

Holding your baby skin-to-skin is one of the most beneficial things you can do for both of you in the early weeks. Skin-to-skin contact lowers stress hormones and releases oxytocin from the anterior pituitary in the brain, causing feelings of warmth, safety, and connection. Remember our discussion of co-regulation? When moms hold babies skin-to-skin, tummy-to-tummy on their chest, babies feel safest. They co-regulate with their mom's nervous system. Babies have access to the familiar rhythms they have known from the very beginning—the rhythm of their mother's breathing, her heartbeat, the sound of her voice, her smell, and the warmth of her skin. Research shows that the best place for babies to be immediately after birth is their mom's chest in a vertical position between her breasts. This is the best place for babies to begin their transition from intrauterine to extrauterine life.

Babies' bodies go through a lot during labor and birth. Their entire circulatory system must transition from receiving oxygen and nourishment from the placenta to filling their lungs with air for the first time and managing all their vital signs independently. When placed skin-to-skin following birth, babies can regulate and stabilize their heart rate, respiratory rate, and temperature. They also initiate and establish breastfeeding more quickly successfully.[6]

There are other important biological factors worth mentioning. Moms and babies are designed to sync and support each other. Moms benefit from skin-to-skin, having their babies close enough to kiss and smell. Stress levels for both mom and baby decrease, and bonding begins. The importance of skin-to-skin contact does not end after the first two hours following birth, also known as the "golden hour." Skin-to-skin contact remains beneficial for baby's brain growth, development, and nervous system regulation during the first few months, and it continues to be important throughout the first year of life.

A few more words about God's incredible biological design: The maternal areola darkens and enlarges during pregnancy, and after birth, glands around the areola secrete a smell similar to that of the amniotic fluid that surrounded the baby in utero. These two factors help baby to be drawn to the breast to nurse. When placed vertically on the mom's chest after birth, babies exhibit a stepping reflex. This is protective for mom, as the baby's stepping movements massage the uterus, helping it contract and clamp down and control postpartum bleeding. When the baby latches and suckles, this stimulation releases oxytocin from the maternal brain, also causing uterine contractions that help shrink the uterus after the birth, protecting the mother from excessive blood loss after delivery.[7]

When you understand how breastfeeding is designed to work, you can set realistic expectations, understand how to tell if your baby is nursing well and getting enough milk, and know how to respond. With breastfeeding, we cannot see how much volume babies are consuming, so we must rely on outward signs to guide us. Learning your baby's sucking patterns will help you determine if your baby is actively transferring milk and getting enough volume.

Managing Challenges and Unmet Expectations

God is our refuge and strength,
a very present help in trouble.
Psalm 46:1

YOU MADE IT. You worked so hard for this very moment. You dreamed of what it would look like and how you would feel—hearing your baby's first cry, feeling their warm skin against your chest, studying each tiny and perfect feature. Adrenaline and oxytocin are swirling, and you are experiencing the initial bond and infinite love for your baby. The birth of your baby is unlike anything else you will experience in life. Let me tell you, as someone who has been a labor and delivery nurse for years and witnessed the miracle of childbirth every time I stepped into work, it never gets old. It is truly miraculous and wondrous, and frankly, it blows my mind to think about how God perfectly designed our bodies to develop our precious babies—from conception through each trimester of pregnancy, the stages of labor, birth, and then breastfeeding. God created our bodies to nourish and nurture our babies through each stage of their growth and development.

When we stop and reflect on this reality and the intricacy, we can't help but be in awe. I would spend hours helping laboring mamas through their pain, uncertainty, and self-doubt. I would encourage, uplift, massage backs and legs, get ice chips, wet washcloths for foreheads while immersing myself in unwavering support of my patients as they labored to bring their babies earthside. What an experience it was to be in such a vulnerable time and space with women and families. Supporting and encouraging as so many women birthed their babies—from the first sight of the fetal head crowning to witnessing the complete joy and awe as women clutched their sweet babies to their chests. The emotions in the room were thick and raw. What a relief and experience it was to be a part of birth repeatedly with every shift I worked.

The Golden Hour

The Golden Hour consists of the first hour or two after birth. The baby is transitioning from intrauterine to extrauterine life. Their safe space is their mom's chest. They sync up with their mom as their co-regulator to stabilize their heart rate, breathing, and temperature. This is usually their most alert time within the first twenty-four hours, which is why it is best to have them placed here immediately following birth, if possible, with proximity to the breast to encourage them to latch and have their first feeding during this time. Babies can initiate breastfeeding more quickly and more successfully when placed skin-to-skin with mom. Mom and baby can feel each other's warmth and touch, which helps lower both of their stress hormones. The release of oxytocin stimulated by breastfeeding also triggers the uterus to contract, helping control postpartum bleeding for mom, which is also very important and protective during the immediate postpartum period.

The Golden Hour is sacred, and it is vital to try to protect it as best we can. Now, there are times that it needs to be interrupted briefly or cannot be completed on mom's chest due to medical necessity. However, if it is at all possible, we want to allow baby to transition to life outside the womb while having close skin-to-skin contact and the familiarity of their mama's voice, the rhythm of her breathing, and her heartbeat. The brain recognizes things that are familiar and rhythmic as being safe. Each pregnancy, labor, and birth experience is unique. It may look exactly how you planned it or imagined, and it may not, and that is okay. The process can be very unpredictable.

The important thing to remember when things are not going as planned or your expectations of your birth experience are slipping away, is knowing what the next step is and staying positive in the moment. Our bodies have a special way of telling us when something isn't going right and we need to pivot. It does not mean that all is lost, or you failed, or that you won't be able to bond or breastfeed if you miss out on the Golden Hour.

You might be in a situation where you need to have a C-section, or your baby might need extra help after the birth or be admitted to the NICU. You might be an adoptive mom who was not able to be present at the birth. I have walked with moms through each of these scenarios and have also experienced one of them myself.

Time to Pivot

I woke up the morning of June 18, 2018, full of excitement and anticipation. I was in early labor with my fourth baby. I went about my morning as usual—getting the kids breakfast, getting them ready for swim practice, and preparing for my thirty-eight-week OB appointment scheduled for late morning. I was so excited to be in labor during the day. With my other three, I labored overnight. Throughout the morning, the contractions were getting consistent but still totally manageable. My doctor checked my cervix at my appointment, and I was 4-5 centimeters. I was still managing fine, and the baby's heartbeat sounded great, so I went home, planning to take the kids to swim practice to help distract me. By the time I was loading the kids into the car, I felt like I should go to the hospital instead. I went back inside and started packing (I have no idea why I didn't already have things ready to go; he was my fourth baby!). My husband called his sister to see if she could meet us at the hospital to pick up the kids while I was getting admitted. I was 6 centimeters when I checked in. The contractions were consistent, stronger, and more frequent. I thought for sure I was going to meet my baby soon. I had planned to labor and deliver without an epidural or IV pain medications, as I had been able to do with my previous two babies. I thought this sweet baby was going to come quickly and easily.

Upon admission around 4:00 p.m., things were already taking an unexpected turn. My blood pressure was elevated, and my lab work showed a low platelet count. I was shocked. I knew what these numbers meant—preeclampsia. Preeclampsia is a serious pregnancy complication that can occur any time after twenty weeks gestation or during the postpartum period. It is characterized by persistent high blood pressure and either protein found in the urine or new onset of low platelet levels, trouble with liver or kidney function, fluid in the lungs, or visual disturbances or seizures. How could this be happening to me? My pregnancy had been completely uncomplicated and healthy. My blood pressure had been completely normal just a few hours before at my appointment in the office. They repeated my labs a couple hours later, and the numbers were worsening.

I had a very consistent and strong contraction pattern when my nurse came in to inform me of my labs, and my doctor broke my water to see if we could speed up the arrival of my sweet babe. Soon after, I was dilated to 9 centimeters. It was intense and hard. My body wanted to deliver my baby, but my cervix wouldn't fully dilate and thus started to swell. I was stalled at 9 centimeters for four hours, laboring, praying, changing positions, trying to move, praying more, and doing everything I could to will my body to allow me to deliver my baby. I remember looking at my husband and my mom and saying, "I can't do this; something is wrong."

It was time to pivot and accept that he would be born with assistance through C-section. Sweet Jack arrived safely in the early morning hours of June 19. The C-section crushed me and was not at all what I had envisioned. I was heartbroken. I was not able to hold my baby skin-to-skin until a few hours after his birth. After he was born, he was handed to the nurse and placed on the radiant warmer to have an assessment and vital signs checked. My husband was able to hold him swaddled in a warm blanket for the duration of my surgery. I held him to my chest as soon as I got the chance, and he latched and breastfed like a champ. I had experience breastfeeding three other babies, which greatly helped my confidence and ability to latch and breastfeed him after my C-section. I think it would have been a totally different story and struggle if this had been my first birth experience. I still grieved the experience I had for quite some time.

One of the things that helped me was thinking about how my disappointment made me a better nurse. I, myself, had an unexpected change in my birth plan, and my expectations were dashed. I was able to better empathize with the patients I cared for who had similar circumstances because I had been there. God is the great Redeemer, and He can restore everything in its time (1 Peter 5; Deut. 30:3). I encourage moms to hold their babies skin-to-skin as soon as possible and as much as they can for the first four weeks of their baby's life outside the womb. It is beneficial in so many ways for both mom and babe. I also encourage moms to tell their story or write their story in a journal to help them process and heal.

Unmet expectations can be damaging and traumatic. We often build something up so much in our heads, imagining over and over how amazing it is going to be, only to be caught off guard when the wind gets knocked out of us. This grief and great loss are compounded and destroy us even more as we are flooded with everyone else's perfect presentation of their life events and circumstances on social media. I have witnessed many different unexpected challenges arise during labor, birth, and initiating breastfeeding. Many factors can impact successful breastfeeding from the very beginning. The labor and birth process, the gestational age of the baby, and the size of the baby, to name a few. Rather than walk into the situation blindly, we must understand certain challenges and how and when to appropriately intervene to protect the breastfeeding relationship.

Gestational age (how many weeks pregnant you are when you give birth) can impact a baby's development and stamina, and can make it difficult for them to breastfeed effectively. NICU admissions complicate breastfeeding as they create a separation between mom and baby, which can delay stimulation of milk supply and cause increased stress hormones. Breech births, cesarean sections, or vacuum- or forceps-assisted deliveries can also impact breastfeeding, as the baby may experience body tension that makes positioning and latching difficult or disrupts their suck-swallow-breathe coordination. It is important to understand that challenges can still arise even after an ideal birth experience and skin-to-skin contact with baby during the Golden Hour. There are cases where difficulties need to be managed so that new moms can breastfeed successfully for as long as they wish.

Hand Expression

One key tool I teach new moms to help them gain confidence and get off to the right start is hand expression. It is one the most important skills for all new moms (ideally taught prenatally). Expressing milk before birth (with their midwife or obstetrician's permission) can be beneficial in case intervention is needed. I also encourage moms to hand express each time they latch their baby in the first three to five days for multiple reasons. Hand expression is particularly useful during the initial engorgement phase and again during the weaning phase.

Hand expression prior to latching your new baby is highly beneficial. First of all, it mobilizes the colostrum, so your baby doesn't have to wait long to get the first drop. By massaging and hand expressing, you "prime the pump" to bring the colostrum closer to the nipple pore, or even to the nipple face, allowing your baby to experience the instant gratification of tasting the colostrum upon latching. This helps baby relax and establish a rhythmic, active nursing pattern more quickly. This tool is especially helpful if you have a sleepy baby. You can even express drops of colostrum directly onto your baby's lips or into their mouth to help wake them up and encourage them to latch and nurse. Even just a few drops in their mouth absorbs quickly to help raise their blood sugar.

Another key benefit to hand expressing each time you prepare to latch and feed your baby in the early days is that it provides more stimulation to the breast, helping to establish and stimulate milk supply. If a baby is too sleepy to latch, expressing milk ensures that your body is still receiving frequent signals to increase milk production. Additionally, some moms report less nipple pain with initial latch when they hand express prior to nursing. The baby can relax sooner as they get a quick taste of colostrum, their jaw doesn't stay so tight, and they do not have to suck as vigorously trying to mobilize the colostrum.

It's also important to note that, just like every pregnancy, labor, and birth can vary, every lactation and breastfeeding experience can be different. For example, I had very different challenges with my first two babies that made it difficult for me to reach my goals with breastfeeding, but with my third baby, everything went smoothly. He latched easily from the start, and I did not have any struggles with my milk supply. I think this was due to the knowledge I gained from my first two experiences; I had less stress since I knew more of what to expect. Stay positive and be confident. Try not to worry, and allow your intuition to guide you. Snuggle and enjoy your baby, nurture them, and love them. There is help and guidance available if you need it, but remember you are exactly what your baby needs.

Let's walk through the steps of hand expression:

1. Lightly massage your breast with one hand on top of the breast and one hand on the bottom. Massage in gentle circular motions. Then, move your hands to either side of the breast and repeat, feeling for glandular tissue. It will feel a little bumpy or spongy. Next, mobilize the entire breast by lifting it gently in clockwise and counterclockwise circles.

2. Place your index finger and thumb of the same hand opposite each other at the edges of the areola.

3. Gently push your breast back against your chest wall, then squeeze your finger and thumb together. It may take thirty to sixty seconds of hand expression before you start to see drops of colostrum. Be patient, don't stress, and relax. It is a learned skill and can take a bit to get the hang of it. Colostrum is stored in the milk ducts back in the glandular breast tissue. Think of it as an accordion that needs to be compressed and squeezed to push the milk out.

4. Every fifteen to thirty seconds, switch breasts.

5. If colostrum is easily expressible, collect it with a colostrum collection kit, or simply express into a medicine cup and draw up into 1 milliliter syringes. Cap the syringes and freeze them in a breastmilk storage bag for later use.

6. Antenatal hand expression practice should be limited to once a day for about five to ten minutes, with permission from your midwife or obstetrician.

The main goal of practicing hand expression antenatally is for practice and gaining confidence in how to express your own milk. The goal is not to collect tons of colostrum. Remember, colostrum is produced in very small volumes, so even expressing just a few beads of colostrum at the nipple is a great achievement. It is okay if you do not see any colostrum when practicing. It is a learned skill and takes time.

Hand expression is a very helpful skill to learn. These are the main reasons why I teach hand expression:

1. It helps you gain confidence in your body's ability to produce breast milk.

2. It familiarizes you with your own breast tissue and how to express milk. It also helps to be familiar with your breasts in case you feel something different in the breast tissue that you hadn't felt before.

3. It is a useful technique to perform prior to every nursing session or pumping session. It increases overall milk production by 60 percent when incorporated in the first few days postpartum.

4. Hand expression prior to latching mobilizes the colostrum to make it quicker and easier for newborns to transfer more colostrum and settle into their active suck/swallow pattern more quickly.

5. It can be used during the engorgement phase to help relieve pressure, especially used in conjunction with lymphatic drainage massage.

6. It is helpful during the weaning process to release pressure and express just enough milk for comfort.

If you are unsure if you are doing it correctly, or if you are having difficulty, reach out and make an appointment with a lactation consultant for help. Hand expression is a very helpful skill to learn prior to babe's arrival.

My breastfeeding journey with my third baby was my first fully successful journey. I felt more confident from everything I had learned in my prior experiences, and I was determined to reach my goals. My labor with Joshua Joel (JJ) was fast and smooth. From the moment my eyes met his, I remember his big brown eyes—he was calm, alert, and quiet, even after his rapid birth. I held him skin-to-skin, and he latched easily and quickly on the first attempt. We started off on the right foot and we never looked back. We did not experience any difficulties with latching, weight gain, or low milk supply. I felt so much more confident and relaxed as we began our feeding journey. I had educated myself on biological normal newborn feeding behavior. I understood how to pump and the importance of frequent and effective milk removal to help establish and maintain my milk supply. This included how to manage and sustain it with my return to work when he was twelve weeks old. We did it. He was a happy and healthy baby and was very easygoing.

Remember, even if your birth doesn't go according to your plan or vision, it will be okay. Focus on the next step. Remember how beneficial skin-to-skin holding is for you and your baby to sync. It helps both mom and baby to lower stress, increase bonding, and have successful feedings. If difficulties in latching persist, knowing the steps and having a plan for appropriate intervention is a necessity. Stay confident, breathe deep, and move forward.

The Importance of Reflexive Latching Technique

I praise you, for I am fearfully and wonderfully made.
Wonderful are your works; my soul knows it very well.
Psalm 139:14

BREASTFEEDING IS NATURAL, but it doesn't always come naturally. I once had a client call me after she was discharged from the hospital, in tears because her baby was not latching at all. She was so discouraged and upset. She had assumed that since she had prepared and learned so much about the labor and delivery process, breastfeeding would just come naturally, and she would learn everything else she needed to know while she was in the hospital. She was caught completely off guard by how challenging and stressful breastfeeding could be.

Breastfeeding is partly innate and partly learned. Babies are born with reflexes that help them feed well to survive. As breastfeeding mothers, it is vital that we understand how to position both ourselves and our baby, and how to trigger the baby's reflexes in the right order to ensure an optimal latch and a successful breastfeeding session. To do so, it is important for both mother and baby to feel safe, secure, and calm, which encourages the release of hormones necessary for breastfeeding and helps the baby use their reflexes to feed well.

I teach a mother-led, reflexive latching technique, especially crucial during the first few days as both mother and baby are learning to nurse together. I teach this technique for two key reasons:

1. It helps the baby achieve a deep latch, which will lead to adequate milk transfer for baby and proper stimulation of the mother's breast tissue to establish a full milk supply.
2. It protects the mother's nipples from visible trauma and excessive pain. While some soreness and tenderness are common at the start of breastfeeding, persistent pain and visible damage are not normal and indicate that something is wrong.

Understanding the newborn reflexes that were designed and hard-wired into their brains to be present at birth will help them latch and feed well. When we trigger these reflexes in the correct sequence, the baby's brain knows what to expect and can anticipate the next reflex, making it easier for them to latch and feed properly. Slowing down and following each step carefully will help both mom and baby to feel confident and secure enough to tap into these innate reflexes. Understanding the biological design behind breastfeeding allows the process to be more intuitive and less stressful. Whether breastfeeding or bottle-feeding, understanding newborn reflexes is crucial.

Newborn Feeding Reflexes

Rooting: When something touches baby's cheek, they turn their head toward it, helping them find the breast.

Gape: When you drag the nipple (breast or bottle) downward from baby's nose to chin, the reflex triggers baby to tilt their head back and open their mouth.

Suck: Triggered when something (such as a finger, pacifier, bottle, or breast) stimulates the baby's hard palate. This reflex helps the baby latch and begin sucking.

These reflexes work in order, helping the baby's brain organize when hungry or upset. Proper positioning is key: If either the mother or baby is uncomfortable, it becomes difficult to trigger these reflexes. Babies need to know where they are in space and how close they are to the breast (rooting reflex). Getting baby to open their mouth wide is essential for achieving a deep latch (gaping reflex). The latch and suck (sucking reflex) will not happen if baby's positioning is off. This can impact the angle of their neck flexion/extension and position of the nipple on the palate.

Anatomy of the Latch

As baby first latches, the nipple touches their hard palate, triggering the sucking reflex. As the baby continues to suckle, the nipple extends and reaches their soft palate. (This is why the toe-curling pain should decrease significantly within the first 30 seconds of active nursing. The sucking pattern allows the nipple and areolar to extend.) Let's try an exercise demonstration: Press your tongue to the roof of your mouth. Your tongue is touching your hard palate. From there, keep your tongue on the roof of your mouth and slide your tongue backward toward your throat until you notice a change in the firmness of your palate. When it feels soft, you know you have reached the soft palate. This is where the nipple is positioned: at the junction of the hard and soft palate with an adequate latch during active nursing. If the pain does not go away after the first thirty seconds of active nursing, the latch is too shallow, and the nipple is not able to reach the baby's soft palate. It is important in the early days especially to assess how the latch looks and feels. We must understand the process to determine if the latch is adequate or needs adjustments.

Let's also keep in mind anatomy of the breast and how milk is adequately removed and transferred to the baby. At the breast, the baby creates an airtight vacuum seal with their tongue when latching adequately. When the latch is deep enough, there is a combination of compression and vacuum as the baby nurses to optimally remove milk. If baby's latch is shallow (just on the nipple) there will be minimal milk transfer, if any at all. The nipple will be repetitively compressed on the baby's hard palate, leading to nipple pain and trauma.

The breast is mostly made up of fat, lymph nodes, and glandular tissue, which contains the alveoli, or lobules, where breast milk is stored. These structures resemble clusters of grapes throughout the breast tissue. The lactiferous ducts are connected from the lobules and end at the lactiferous sinus or nipple pore where the milk exits the nipple face. Women have multiple nipple pores that can range from four to twenty. The areola is the area surrounding the nipple where the Montgomery glands are located. These glands secrete oils to keep the nipple and areola moisturized. The secretions are believed to have the same scent as the amniotic fluid, helping to draw baby to the nipple after birth. The areola also darkens and becomes enlarged to stand out easier to baby, since their vision is blurry and they can only see contrast at first.[8]

How to Set Up for Latching

Babies need to feel safe, secure, and connected when positioning for latching. Mom also needs to be comfortable and confident in her own positioning. Baby cannot be in a fight-or-flight nervous system state and simultaneously trigger their suck reflex. Having a set of steps to follow when first learning how to position and latch baby to the breast—steps that align with their nervous system and innate reflexes—can be helpful. Experiment with sitting in different chairs, couches, or beds until you find the right spot. I recommend practicing deep breathing, rolling your shoulders, relaxing, and massaging your breast while hand-expressing to mobilize milk before attempting to latch the baby.

Babies use their entire body to breastfeed—not just their mouth. This is why optimal body positioning for both mom and baby is of vital importance. Baby's and mom's bodies work together to breastfeed. If positioning is off, babies are more likely to enter a fight-or-flight response, which prevents them from engaging the reflexes that help them latch effectively. Likewise, if mom is stressed, this can also make it harder for the baby to latch properly. Babies co-regulate with their mom, and their vital signs and stress hormones synchronize. Research shows that when babies are skin-to-skin on mom's chest, their heart rate, respiratory rate, and temperature regulate. Stress hormones decrease for mom and baby as oxytocin is released with skin-to-skin contact. Gently patting baby's bum while making a quiet shushing sound can also help calm baby prior to latching. Occasionally, it can be beneficial to pass baby to a support person if one is available so you can "reset," get a breath, and try again.

It's okay to switch chairs if a feeding isn't going well. I encourage mom to stand, soothe baby, take a drink of water, and then try again in another chair.

Breastfeeding pillows are meant to support mom's arm, not just the baby. I have found that these pillows sometimes make optimal positioning more challenging because they can become a crutch, preventing mom's and baby's bodies from fully communicating with each other. They can restrict the baby's closeness and movement, making the experience feel stagnant, rigid, and almost forced. Without freedom of movement, the baby is less able to achieve an optimal latch, and the mother's ability to adjust the baby's position is limited. Baby needs to be as close as possible to mom, with skin-to-skin contact, and held assertively but gently. The physical closeness helps baby feel safe and allows for the deepest possible latch. Skin-to-skin contact also lowers stress hormones, prompting a sense of calm for both mom and baby. When the pair is calm and relaxed, baby feels safe and latches easier, and mom's oxytocin flows more freely, enhancing milk production and flow.

Breastfeeding in the first few days versus four weeks down the line can look completely different. In the beginning, both mom and baby are learning, so careful attention to positioning and latching techniques can be very beneficial for setting up successful feedings. As breastfeeding continues, it becomes easier and quicker as confidence and muscle memory grow. Baby will latch without much direction from mom and will be able to maintain their latch and milk transfer more efficiently. Try not to feel discouraged in the early days and weeks of breastfeeding. It will get easier—and if it does not, be sure to reach out for help and guidance.

Comfortable, high-quality nursing bras or nursing camisoles can make latching easier. Camisoles with clip-down tops allow for discreet nursing if that is important to you. Nursing scarves or muslin blankets can serve as cover-ups if you prefer or need to nurse modestly in certain locations or situations. A well-fitting, comfortable bra makes nursing less cumbersome, and you do not have to worry about fussing with your clothing as you concentrate on helping your baby latch. I recommend having both clip-down bras and soft, crisscross sleep nursing bras.

One-hundred percent cotton breast pads can be useful when milk passively leaks from breasts during feedings and whenever oxytocin is released, causing the milk ejection reflex. This sensitivity in early postpartum causes copious milk leaking. It continues to occur until your body downregulates for the first time, around the two-week postpartum mark. Keeping burp cloths nearby while nursing can help manage the excess milk, which can make latching slippery and difficult. Several passive milk collectors are now available on the market that can be worn inside a bra to help keep the area dry while also collecting a little extra milk to use later.

I recommend nipple balms that include calendula in the ingredient list due to the anti-inflammatory properties of the herb, along with organic coconut oil, which has natural antifungal properties, and Medihoney, which is ultra-pasteurized and ultrafiltered. Silver nipple covers can also be beneficial for healing and reducing nipple tenderness. If using silver nipple covers, no additional balms or creams are necessary.

The Optimal Latch

Here is a simple technique to help you and baby master the art of the latch. It may be beneficial to use a mirror or enlist the help of your partner or lactation consultant to get these steps down:

1. Always gently massage the breast and hand express colostrum to "prime the pump." This mobilizes the colostrum to the tip of the nipple prior to latching. Baby can settle into an active nursing pattern more quickly when they do not have to work so hard to pull the first few drops of colostrum. It also is a great intervention to help sleepy babies nurse more effectively.

2. Support your baby's back with your forearm and their head by positioning the "V" between your thumb and index finger where the base of their neck and top of shoulders meet.

3. Support the baby with your right arm and right hand when latching on the left side and your left hand will support your left breast.

4. Position the baby on their side and check that their ear, shoulder, and hip are all in alignment. They should have their tummy turned in toward you. Their bottom arm should be tucked underneath the breast and both arms should come

around the breast in a hug. This will allow for the baby to get as close to you as possible to achieve the deep latch.

5. Hold them securely and with assertiveness so they feel safe and supported. This helps them trigger their reflexes to achieve an optimal latch.

6. Line baby up with their nose at your nipple. Drag the nipple from their nose to bottom lip to trigger them. Baby will reflexively tilt their head back and open their mouth.

7. Once baby fully opens their mouth, quickly and firmly bring the center of baby's mouth over the middle of the nipple while their chin reaches your breast. Simultaneously, use your hand to squeeze the breast tissue while baby latches deeply into the breast.

8. Always bring baby to the breast when latching; do not try to just aim yourself into the baby's mouth.

9. Do not force your baby or push their head straight into the breast. Their reflexes need to be triggered to allow them to anticipate the breast.

10. Hold the breast support and breathe through the first thirty seconds, assessing how the latch feels and watching baby's sucking pattern.

11. When baby is latched well and actively in a sucking pattern, lean back and get comfortable. You do not need to continue to hold breast support unless baby's latch slips when you let go. Baby will get stronger and be able to maintain latch by themselves in one to two weeks, if not sooner.

This latching technique is especially beneficial in the early days, when mom and baby are learning and feedings are frequent, to prevent nipple damage and ensure effective milk transfer. Latching may not always look like this, or be this involved, but it is a foundational starting point to ensure breastfeeding has the best chance of success.

Is My Baby Eating Enough?

Gracious words are like a honeycomb, sweetness
to the soul and health to the body.
Proverbs 16:24

BREASTFEEDING CAN CAUSE anxiety and worry, especially when it comes to uncertainty about how baby is doing. Moms may feel overwhelmed by the advice they receive from social media, friends, and family, which isn't always accurate or helpful. This often stems from a lack of understanding about what is common, though not always correct, versus what is normal and expected. There are ways to simplify and concentrate on what you know to be helpful and true.

Prenatal lactation education is vital. Understanding what to look for to determine whether your baby is having quality feedings is invaluable for building confidence in breastfeeding from the very beginning. It can be hard to grasp and maintain new information when you are already exhausted, sore, and worried about your baby. Fortunately, prenatal lactation consultations and breastfeeding classes are available from most lactation consultants and may be covered by insurance.

There are some tangible ways that I can teach you how to answer some very common questions I hear almost every day. Let me answer a couple of these questions:

1. How can I tell my baby is getting enough milk?
2. How can I tell when my baby is finished during a nursing session?

Recognizing Sucking Patterns

Recognizing your baby's sucking patterns will help you determine the quality of their feeding. It's difficult to know the exact volume of milk baby is drinking during breastfeeding. This is why it is so beneficial to understand how to assess the outward signs that tell you baby is drinking enough milk for optimal growth.

Learning to recognize baby's sucking patterns will help you decide what phase of nursing your baby is currently in and whether they are actively swallowing milk. This will also guide you in knowing when to unlatch and offer the other side, or when to end the feeding. This is especially important in the early days when milk transfer is critical for baby's growth and establishing a full milk supply.

The first two weeks are crucial for establishing milk supply. Adequate stimulation and milk removal in the first fourteen days postpartum directly correlates with how much milk your body will continue to produce to sustain an exclusive breastfeeding relationship.

Often, when moms struggle with low milk supply at two to four weeks postpartum, it's due to mismanaged feeding difficulties or a lack of understanding of how breastfeeding is established in the first two weeks. This is usually caused by infrequent or ineffective stimulation and milk removal.

If you suspect low milk supply or your baby is struggling to gain weight, it would be highly beneficial to work with an IBCLC to help identify the root cause and develop a plan to get things back on track. I *love* when moms are able to find hope through a plan that helps them achieve their breastfeeding goals. When I was a young mom, I wish I had known I could reach out for help when things weren't working in my first breastfeeding experience. I needed someone to give me actionable steps to continue the journey. The relief I see on a mother's face when we identify the problem and create a plan is what keeps me doing what I do every day.

Active Nursing

During colostrum feedings, look for an adequate latch followed by what we call a "burst" of sucking (five to ten sucks in a row), followed by a short pause and the jaw dropping downward and extending or lengthening. You may or may not hear a tiny little "cuh" sound simultaneous with the jaw drop. This indicates a swallow. Baby should then go back into their sucking burst, followed by another swallow.

Once mature milk transitions in—typically between three to five days postpartum—the suck-to-swallow ratio decreases, and feedings become more efficient. Look for a 1:1, 2:1, or 3:1 suck-to-swallow ratio. As milk volume increases, milk transfer also increases, and the suck-to-swallow ratio becomes smaller. It is much easier to determine swallows when the volume of milk is higher.

Comfort Nursing

Comfort nursing, or passive nursing, occurs when baby suckles lightly and is not actively pulling milk. During the colostrum phase, there will be long pauses between swallows or sucking bursts. Babies convert to this type of sucking pattern when they are sleepy or trying to stimulate another letdown after mature milk has transitioned in.

Once the milk lets down, the baby will return to an active, rhythmic suck/swallow pattern with very frequent swallows.

Comfort nursing (and specifically the peristalsis of the tongue during comfort nursing) helps babies' digestive process, helps to move gas through, and helps them poop. Comfort nursing is important for babies' soothing and sleep. If you are unsure whether your baby has finished nursing, try stimulating them back into the active nursing phase. The best way to do this is by doing breast compressions or by rubbing your baby's back, feet, or ear to stimulate them to wake up and begin an active and rhythmic suck/swallow pattern again. If baby continues comfort nursing despite stimulation, they are finished nursing. You can rest assured that they drank enough milk and are satisfied with this feeding.

It is important to recognize the different sucking patterns when trying to determine if baby is getting enough milk to grow and gain weight appropriately. In the first two weeks, babies usually want to nurse every two to three hours to help them regain their birth weight. This also builds and establishes a full milk supply. The frequency of stimulation, along with effective and quality feedings, helps ensure milk supply is sufficiently established moving forward in the breast-feeding journey.

Outward Signs of Adequate Milk Intake

What are some of the outward signs we can look for to verify baby is getting enough milk and nursing well?

1. Latch looks and feels good.
2. Active sucking patterns are present during feedings.
3. Swallows are visible or audible.
4. Baby is content, sleepy, or quiet/alert after feedings.

5. Diaper output is adequate (at least 6-7 wet diapers and 3-4 stools per 24 hours after day five; stools may decrease after four weeks).

6. Weight gain is appropriate (approximately 0.5-1 ounce per day after the initial weight loss has subsided, until about three months old).

7. In some cases, blood sugar and bilirubin levels may be assessed.

Offering the breast every time the baby cues, and at least every two to three hours during the first couple of weeks, is critical. This helps establish a full milk supply and provides baby with frequent, consistent nutrition for growth and development, and also frequent nurturing and bonding. Feeding on demand is beneficial. This is how breastfeeding was designed and created to work. Baby is designed to go to the breast to signal mom's body to continue producing milk or increase the amount of milk. Scheduled feedings get in the way of how the relationship is designed to function. We risk low milk supply or slow weight gain when we try to control when, or how often, baby is put to the breast.

Don't Go It on Your Own

The early days with a newborn can be exhausting as everyone adjusts to new rhythms. Keep in mind, this season will eventually pass. Give yourself grace upon grace and reach out for help and support as needed. Rest when you can, eat nourishing foods, and hydrate well. A supportive lactation consultant can help you navigate the early days and weeks of learning breastfeeding, infant cues, and newborn care. She will offer encouragement and emotional support, and give you peace of mind as she teaches you and answers all your questions. Nothing can replace support that is constant; someone you can count on when challenges and uncertainty make you second-guess your intuition.

Breastfeeding can take many forms, and there are various ways to support mom and baby. Care plans and feeding plans are often put into place to help meet the needs of mom and baby. If mom is struggling with sleep deprivation that is impacting her mental health, the care plan can be adjusted to include pumping and bottle-feeding sessions. This can give mom a mental break if needed and allow dad to bond with baby through bottle-feeding. I always remind parents that breastfeeding is never an all-or-nothing decision; there are always alternatives when needed. Lactation consultants can help create a solid feeding plan that protects mom's milk supply and allows the baby to get the nourishment they need, whether through breastfeeding, bottle-feeding, or a combination of both. Every situation is unique, and it is important for parents to know that it is okay to discuss challenges and seek support.

I once worked with a very special mother and baby, whom I ultimately counseled to stop pumping and switch to donor milk and formula feeding. Although I have permission to share their story, for privacy reasons, we will call the mom "Amber" and the baby "Billy." Amber was incredibly dedicated and persevered through many challenges. Her sweet baby, Billy, was born prematurely via cesarean section due to medical complications. Amber began pumping immediately and was diligent in trying to increase her milk supply. She followed every recommendation she received on how to establish and maintain her supply while Billy was in the NICU and unable to breastfeed. She was, and still is, the best possible mom for Billy.

She was pumping around the clock but yielding very little output. Her milk supply never fully transitioned, and she continued to produce only 10 to 20 milliliters per pumping session. The stress began to wear on her emotionally and physically. It began to impact her bonding with her sweet son. Every time she pumped, she was reminded that she was not able to produce the total volume of milk he needed to grow.

We had an open and honest conversation about her feelings, and I reassured her that it was okay to stop. I validated her experience, encouraged her, and reminded her that she was amazing; she did everything possible to provide Billy with all the milk her body was able to produce. I told her that every drop truly mattered—each ounce she had given him helped him grow stronger and provided vital nourishment and protection. Because of the trust and rapport we had built, Amber was able to make the best decision for her and her baby—without guilt or shame.

Sometimes, a care plan needs to change, and that is okay. No one is locked into a single approach. Talk through your situation and with someone you trust—someone who has your best interest at heart. Sometimes you need someone to be honest with you and hold your hand through heavy decision making.

Amber and I became friends about three years later when she reached out to thank me. She told me that my guidance helped save her life during that challenging and emotional time. God orchestrates our lives, relationships, and encounters. We usually don't see it in the moment, but we can look back and undoubtedly see His loving plan. To this day, Amber and I are very close, and I know God didn't bring us together by mistake.

You Don't Know What You Don't Know

For the Lord gives wisdom, from His mouth
come knowledge and understanding.
Proverbs 2:6

"I JUST DIDN'T KNOW." I hear this phrase every day. There is much to know and understand, and unfortunately, finding correct, beneficial, and easily comprehensible information can be challenging. Conflicting information is everywhere and it can be difficult to determine what is correct when you are exhausted and scouring the internet for answers.

Many women have told me breastfeeding didn't work out with their first baby—they simply did not produce enough milk, or their milk just dried up unexpectedly. With second, third, or fourth pregnancies, mothers seek the education needed to set themselves and their babies up for success. Breastfeeding is time-sensitive, and difficulties within the first two critical weeks of stimulating and establishing milk supply can make it very difficult to recover a full milk supply.

Often, struggles with low milk supply stem from a misunderstanding or mismanagement of early breastfeeding challenges. Knowing when and how to intervene to ensure that baby receives adequate milk and that mom's milk supply is being stimulated and established appropriately are two key factors. There are some medical diagnoses that make it impossible for moms to produce a full milk supply regardless of her efforts. This is why I highly recommend a prenatal lactation consultation with an IBCLC who can assess the situation and create an individualized care plan.

Ignorance Is Not Bliss

As a first-time mom, I had no idea what to expect from labor, birth, breastfeeding, or motherhood. I was too young and naive to realize that it could be hard. I was expectant and full of joy and awe. As I shared in the introduction, my return back to work was the beginning of the end for breastfeeding. After several weeks of being away from my daughter and not pumping consistently, I thought my milk supply simply dried up out of nowhere.

Looking back, I now recognize multiple factors that played a role in my early weaning. First, I had a used breast pump; second, I had an incorrect flange size; and third, I was not pumping to maintain my supply when I was away from my baby. I now know that a prenatal breastfeeding class and a return-to-school consultation would have benefitted me, allowing me to breastfeed Lily longer. I lacked knowledge about milk production, proper pump usage, and maintaining supply while separated from my baby. I did not even know lactation consultants existed. Had I received timely education and support, I could have recovered my supply and established a successful routine of breastfeeding, pumping, and bottle-feeding. My lack of knowledge and resources drove me into this profession. I want all moms to have access to quality education and support to help them reach their goals without being forced to wean prematurely.

Growing in knowledge fosters confidence, and access to ongoing support is vital for mother's success in breastfeeding.

Maintaining Milk Supply

We discussed how to establish milk supply in an earlier chapter; now we turn to maintaining milk supply to ensure you reach your breastfeeding goals. Once milk supply is fully established, frequent and effective milk removal becomes crucial to sustaining it. Every woman's body responds differently to the number of milk removals needed within twenty-four hours to maintain supply. My best advice is to pump every three hours when initially separated from your baby. After observing how your body adjusts and the amount of milk you collect throughout the day, you can modify your pumping schedule as needed.

Mimicking on-demand breastfeeding while away from your baby is challenging. We learned in a previous chapter that babies nurse for reasons beyond just hunger. When they have unrestricted access to breastfeeding and can cue for it throughout the day without a rigid schedule, it helps protect the milk supply. Babies naturally cluster-feed when they need to boost milk supply, and mom's body responds to this biological design. Cluster feeding is when baby cues to nurse more frequently—often every hour for three to four hours in a row—before taking a longer nap. This pattern signals the mother's body to increase milk production.

When moms and babies are separated, a pumping schedule is necessary. I highly recommend working with a skilled IBCLC when preparing to return to work or school. Continuing to follow up with an IBCLC during transition is invaluable, as individualized care is critical—there is no one-size-fits-all approach. Ideally, you should pump around the times your baby usually takes a bottle. If that is not feasible, start by pumping every three hours, beginning from the last milk removal. An IBCLC can help you fine-tune your pumping schedule and ensure you collect the necessary volume for your baby's bottles. It is important to assess the total daily pumped volume rather than focusing on the amount collected per individual session.

Types of Breast Pumps

Breast pumps are useful when baby cannot effectively remove milk from the breast, or when mom and baby are separated. Remember—frequent, effective milk removal is critical for establishing and maintaining supply. A breast pump mimics what baby would do, thus protecting milk supply. If milk remains in the breast too long, it sends a negative feedback signal to the brain, telling it to slow down milk production. If you are concerned that baby is not removing milk well or are unsure whether pumping is necessary, ask a lactation consultant for personalized guidance.

Breast pumps are not always necessary immediately after birth. If baby is latching well, nursing effectively, and gaining weight appropriately, pumping is unnecessary. However, breast pumps can be a helpful tool if extra stimulation is necessary. Pumping right after giving birth is recommended in cases where baby is admitted to the NICU, has continued difficulty latching after twenty-four hours, receives supplementation with donor milk or formula, or when maternal health history warrants extra stimulation to establish the supply.

Researching and choosing a breast pump is an important task prior to babe's arrival. This is great to discuss in a prenatal consult with a lactation consultant. Asking questions and discussing your unique situation can help determine how pumping might fit into your breastfeeding journey. A lactation consultant can help you decide which type of pump best suits your situation.

Most insurance plans will provide you with an electric breast pump at no cost for each baby that you have. There are websites you can order through, or you can simply call your insurance company and ask how to order a breast pump.

Silicone one piece breast pumps have a time and a place, but they need to be used appropriately, as to not create problems. They can cause oversupply and overactive letdown if not used carefully. I never recommend using them on one side while nursing on the first side for a baby with slow or inadequate weight gain. While marketed as passive milk collectors, they extract more milk than just the initial letdown. This is the readily available, easy flowing milk that baby is able to drink without much effort, especially on the second side when baby is getting sleepy. We do not want to take that milk, because they might lose stamina sooner and stop working for the second letdown because they are not being rewarded by the flow of milk that is normally there when switching sides. If you have excessive leaking during letdown, I prefer the simple milk collectors to wear in your bra that do not have suction during nursing. This type of collector does not pull milk away from baby.

The **manual or hand pump** is a great option for quick milk removal with fewer parts to clean. Again, proper flange size is critical, and finding a good rhythm for doing the pulls will help with efficient and effective milk removal. Although manual pumps extract milk from one breast at a time, they are often more efficient than using a double electric pump for fifteen minutes.

The **double electric breast pump** is ideal for establishing and maintaining milk supply due to their powerful motors. The strong motor yields better stimulation and vacuum to remove the milk from the breast effectively and efficiently. I usually recommend this type of pump when working to establish supply and during the initial return to work.

The **wearable breast pump** is ultraconvenient and works well for many people. Some people find it just doesn't remove milk as well as a double electric pump. Proper fit and positioning of the pump within the bra are critical. I always recommend gentle breast massage and hand expression prior to putting on the wearable pump to help mobilize the milk and encourage it to flow easier. The wearable pump is not ideal for establishing milk supply in the first three to four weeks, but can be trialed after this period to assess milk collection efficiency. It works best as a secondary pump when the hands-free option is needed.

Flange Sizing

Proper flange fitting by an IBCLC is essential. The flange is the funnel-shaped component that encases the nipple, allowing it to move in and out during pumping to extract milk. Pumping should never be painful, cause blistering, or result in purple nipples. Correct sizing it critical for comfort and efficient milk removal.

It is most beneficial to do a fitting during a prenatal consultation, ensuring you have the correct equipment if immediate pumping is needed after the baby is born. Flange size is determined by measuring the diameter of the nipple. A proper fit is assessed based on comfort and how the nipple moves withing the flange. Postpartum assessments also consider milk volume collected. Clear silicone flange inserts allow for precise sizing adjustments. Nipple size may change slightly due to hormone changes toward the end of pregnancy, but usually not a huge amount. When I size someone, I usually recommend two flange sizes to have on hand. For example, if prenatally measured at 15 millimeters, you might need 17 millimeters postpartum but not a 24 millimeter.

Lubricating the funnel of the flange with organic coconut oil or nipple balm can be beneficial to help decrease friction and make it more comfortable to pump. Lack of education on pump use and flange fit can add unnecessary stress, especially if feeding difficulties arise in early postpartum. Being prepared with the right knowledge and equipment can make a substantial difference in your breastfeeding journey.

Going Back to Work

Adding a morning pump session between weeks three and four is typically when I recommend beginning to collect milk for storage in preparation for returning to work or school. It is best to pump immediately following the first morning feeding. You will have the most amount of milk first thing in the morning, as prolactin—the milk-producing hormone—surges overnight. Pump both sides simultaneously for 15 minutes, then store the milk away for later. Remember to date and time-stamp all collected milk. Some people prefer to collect and pool milk for several days before transferring it into storage containers for the freezer. This helps distribute nutrients evenly throughout all bottles and decreases the number of containers or bottles of milk in the fridge. It is okay to combine milk from different times of day. It is okay to combine milks of different temperatures (i.e., pouring freshly pumped milk immediately into the pooled milk container in the fridge) but the instant temperature change may slightly affect the fragile milk cells. This will not harm the baby, but it may slightly reduce the level of potency.

Regarding pump part storage, it's okay to place used pump parts in a gallon-sized zip-lock bag and store them in the refrigerator between pumping sessions to avoid washing after every use. This approach is particularly helpful for those pumping multiple times a day. However, I do not recommend this method if you have a NICU baby, a baby who has had a gut infection, an immunocompromised baby, or if mom has a current yeast or breast infection or has abscess or open wounds on her nipples. Additionally, if a clean environment for handling milk and pump parts is not possible, this method should be avoided. While no solid research exists on this topic, if you do choose the refrigerator storage method, I strongly recommend washing pump parts with soap and water at the end of each day and sterilizing them at least once a week.

Remember, you do not need hundreds of ounces of milk stored in your freezer. You only need enough to get you through the first day away from your baby, because ideally you will be pumping to replace what you used while you were away. The most recently pumped milk is preferable, as it contains the latest antibodies and nutritional composition tailored to your baby's current needs. It is best to have 1-1.25 ounces per hour that you are away from your baby available. When freezing milk, you can pour it into breast milk freezer storage bags, silicone milk storage bags, or even glass jars if you prefer that. Milk can be stored in the refrigerator for four to eight days before needing to be frozen.

For those returning to work or incorporating bottle-feedings at any point, I recommend introducing the bottle around the three- to four-week mark. Begin with a snack-sized feeding of 0.5-1 ounce using a paced bottle-feeding technique, a gradual slope slow-flow nipple, and an upright or side-lying position. The key to bottle-feeding is to ensure a quality feeding experience. The baby's latch should be airtight, with lips flanged outward around the nipple base—resembling a "fishy face." Signs of poor latch include lip puckering, cheek dimpling, clicking sounds, milk dribbling, or distress during feeding. Sometimes, changing the nipple flow or shape is necessary to optimize feeding quality.

Paced bottle-feeding technique is a crucial skill to master when feeding baby bottles at any time because it mimics breastfeeding. Selecting the appropriate nipple shape and flow speed is vital. The goal of paced feeding is to achieve high quality feeding that closely mimics breastfeeding, enabling a smooth transition between breast and bottle while preventing overfeeding. Babies do not experience true nipple confusion; rather, they develop a flow preference. If the flow is too rapid and the baby is in a position where milk flows too quickly, they may consume too much, too fast. Breastfeeding requires more effort, as babies must work to trigger letdowns and transfer milk differently than when bottle-feeding.

Returning to work can feel emotionally, physically, and mentally draining. Give yourself lots of grace and take one day at a time. This transition period is an adjustment, but you will find a new rhythm. Find ways to decompress and rejuvenate. Look at pictures and videos of your baby often if you need to. This can be especially helpful during pumping sessions to help boost oxytocin and milk supply. Spend intentional time reconnecting with your baby when you are reunited. Skin-to-skin contact, co-bathing, snuggling, reading books, nursing, singing, and rocking your baby are all things you can do to help reestablish your connection. Nourish yourself with good food and stay hydrated. Don't forget to add a mineral drink daily to hydrate at the cellular level. (See my favorite mineral drink recipe below.) Finding ways to regulate your nervous system are also highly beneficial. When our bodies function optimally, we feel our best.

Lindsay's mineral drink recipe:

- ½ cup organic, unsweetened coconut water
- ½ cup flavored, unsweetened sparkling water of choice
- Fresh squeeze of lime and/or lemon
- Pinch of pink Himalayan salt

Strategies for Supporting Nervous System Function:

1. Daily morning devotions and prayer
2. Visits to a nervous-system-focused chiropractor
3. Deep breathing exercises

4. Morning sunlight exposure before screen use (or red light therapy)
5. Gentle movement in the morning (stretching, walking, mobility routine)
6. Nutrient-dense breakfast

Milk Storage Guidelines

Milk Storage Guidelines

from the Academy of Breastfeeding Medicine Protocol #8

ROOM TEMPERATURE
16-29 °C AND 60-85 °F

 4 hours optimal,
6-8 hours acceptable

REFRIGERATOR
~4 °C AND 39.2 °F

 4 days optimal,
5-8 days acceptable

FREEZER
<-4 °C AND 29 °F

 6 months optimal,
12 months acceptable

Bottle Feeding

I work with many babies who are bottle-fed exclusively. Parents choose bottle-feeding for a multitude of reasons. In some cases, due to certain medical diagnoses and/or surgeries, moms are not able to breastfeed or produce enough milk for their babies. Some examples include, but are not limited to, lumpectomies, breast reduction surgery, breast implant surgery, mastectomy, polycystic ovarian syndrome (PCOS), hypothyroidism, diabetes, insufficient glandular tissue (IGT), and in vitro fertilization (IVF). These situations do not always result in low milk supply, but they present a higher risk and can require close assessment and management both prenatally and postpartum. Whenever parents choose to bottle-feed, this is absolutely acceptable.

There are many infant formulas on the market, which serve as breast milk substitutes and help babies grow. When donor milk is an option, some parents use a combination of donor milk, formula, and any milk mom can produce. Every family must do what works and feels best for them. Every baby, mom, and family is different and unique. I strongly believe individualized care is essential. When it comes to babies and feeding, there is no single correct answer or protocol that should be applied. There are numerous variables to consider, and exceptional care requires someone who can holistically assess both mom and baby, identify the root cause of challenges or symptoms, and develop and implement specific care plans to alleviate these issues. Bottle-feeding quality is just as important as breastfeeding quality because it can impact baby's comfort, digestion, growth, and sleep, as well as mom's confidence.

I want the bottle-feeding mamas to hear this: You are an amazing mom, and your baby can bond and thrive just as well as if you were breastfeeding. Bottle-feeding does not make you any less of a mom, doesn't mean you failed in any way—and yes, your baby loves you just the same. If you are grieving the loss of breastfeeding when it was your desire, I want you to know that I am truly sorry.

Whether you are currently feeding an infant or are pregnant and preparing for your next journey, I am so glad you are reading this book. My goal is to educate, encourage, and uplift, no matter your situation. I was in your position with my second baby, so I completely empathize. I have walked this path. She is now fifteen, and I can tell you she is absolutely beautiful, smart, creative, talented, securely attached to both my husband and me, and an amazing young woman. Our feeding journey looked different, but our bond and my love for her remained unchanged. Do not listen to the noise and pressures or succumb to the guilt and shame that can feel overwhelming, especially as we navigate motherhood.

I want to discuss the quality of bottle-feeding. The quality of latching onto the bottle is just as important as the quality of latch in breastfeeding. It is essential for babies to have optimal oral function when bottle-feeding to ensure comfort and to prevent symptoms such as reflux, spit-up, gas pains, and overall discomfort. In my practice, I have found that when parents feel confident in their bottle-feeding skills, they experience less stress and can bond with and enjoy feeding their babies more easily. When bottle-feeding is difficult and uncomfortable for the baby, feeding sessions can become unenjoyable, disrupting the release of oxytocin and the feelings of nurture and bonding.

I love working prior to babe's arrival with families who are going to exclusively bottle-feed. Before the baby's arrival, parents learn about appropriate milk volumes per age/size of baby, how to pace feed, how to choose the best bottle, and how to choose infant formula. If applicable, I also educate parents on using their breast pump, covering topics such as setup, usage, cleaning guidelines, optimal milk storage, flange fitting, and how to maximize pump volume output. Preparation and education are critical to starting off on the right foot. Being prepared in advance allows parents to have everything ready to go as soon as baby arrives. Whether a homebirth or in the hospital, they can start bottle-feeding immediately.

Exclusively bottle-fed babies also benefit from skin-to-skin after birth. It is important for them to receive skin-to-skin contact to stabilize vital signs and help them regulate their breathing, decrease stress hormones, and improve bonding and attachment.

Starting with small-volume feedings in a syringe with a finger-feeding technique helps babies develop their suck-swallow-breathe coordination from the beginning. This approach helps protect against overfeeding and poor-quality feedings, which can lead to discomfort for baby and stressful feeding situations. A slip-tip syringe, which has a tapered plastic tip rather than a needle, is ideal for this method. It can easily be inserted into the corner of the baby's mouth when they are sucking on your finger. You can slowly push the milk as baby is sucking to help baby with suck-swallow-breathe coordination. Once baby is consuming over 10 milliliters via syringe and finger-feeding, I recommend switching to bottle-feeding. Syringe and finger-feeding are especially useful during the first 24-48 hours. This is also important for moms who are exclusively pumping and bottle-feeding, as it raises her confidence with the volume she can pump. During our prior discussion of colostrum, remember it is produced in very small, highly concentrated volumes in the beginning—perfect for baby. The small volume works better in a syringe than a bottle. Baby gets used to taking volume more similarly to their biological design when they can mimic colostrum feedings.

When teaching parents to bottle-feed, I encourage a reflexive, baby-led latching approach. Babies organize feeding more effectively when reflexes are triggered in the correct order, allowing them to anticipate the bottle nipple stimulating their hard palate. This method prevents gagging, tongue thrusting, and nipple chewing, which can occur when the nipple is simply pushed into the mouth. Once the baby latches onto the bottle, it's important to assess the latch for width, depth, seal, and comfort, as well as oral function quality during sucking and swallowing. This is where paced feeding comes into play. It is a delicate balance as we watch baby's cues and body language to help determine if feeding is comfortable or a struggle. Baby should be relaxed during feeding and have a rhythmic suck-swallow pattern with breaks for breathing. A general guideline is approximately five minutes per ounce of milk.

Red flags during bottle-feeding include clenched toes, a furrowed brow, tightly fisted hands tucked under baby's chin, milk leaking from the corners of the mouth, clicking sound, the bottle nipple collapsing in baby's mouth, and either excessively fast or slow drinking. Be watchful, ensuring that baby is not losing stamina, getting sleepy, or not completing feedings.

There are many variables that can impact quality bottle-feeding. Most often, I see babies having gassiness, discomfort, excess spit-up, or difficulty having bowel movements—stemming from the latch on the bottle and the quality of feeding. Sometimes the baby's overall body and mouth tension are making it difficult for them to position optimally and to have full range of motion with their tongue. It is important to assess the baby's tension and fascial strain patterns as we work to improve bottle-feeding quality.

Fascia is the connective tissue between the muscles and skin. It is connected in one large sheet from the lingual frenulum all the way down to the toes. Restricted fascia can impact baby's comfort, movement, and range of motion. If the range of motion is limited it can impact positioning, latch, tongue movement, and overall feeding quality. I learned how to recognize tension and fascial strain patterns and how to release them; it completely changed my practice. It deepened my understanding and ability to assess situations more thoroughly and see progress with feeding difficulties that immediately impacted babies' comfort, digestion, overall tension, and rest. I took a special training course that taught me the skills needed to work with ages infant to adult in understanding and recognizing the strain patterns to be able to release them. I highly recommend working with a provider who makes assessments with a full-body approach and who understands on a deep level how to find the root cause of the challenges you are facing.

Fascial strain can be caused by different things. Sometimes it is restricted movement inside the uterus before birth due to low amniotic fluid, multiple fetuses, short or tangled umbilical cord, different uterus shape, or breech position. It can also be related to a rapid labor and birth, or a prolonged labor and birth. If the baby was born via cesarean section, vacuum-assisted, or forceps-assisted births, they might have fascial strain present as well. If your baby struggles with bottle-feeding, seek an evaluation from a provider trained to assess latch, feeding quality, body tension, and oral function. Sometimes, subtle changes can be made like the positioning of baby, what shape and flow rate the bottle nipple is, or the frequency and volume baby is drinking. You and your baby are unique, and you deserve a thorough evaluation by someone who offers support and encouragement to help you both thrive.

If anyone reading this book is struggling with feeling inadequate, confused, overwhelmed, or hopeless, please reach out for support. Pregnancy and postpartum is a wild ride for women due to severe hormone shifts, and physical, spiritual, and emotional changes that occur. Women experience the largest hormone shift during their lifetime in the postpartum period. It's invaluable to have a trusted counselor, friend, sister, mom, spiritual mom, mother-in-law, sister-in-law, lactation consultant, or someone who you align with who can affirm, listen, encourage, and just be there for you.

Managing Challenges

Be strong and courageous. Do not be frightened and do not be dismayed, for the Lord your God Is with you wherever you go.
Joshua 1:9

I T'S 3:00 A.M. Your energy is dangerously low, and you feel utterly depleted. You are caught in the balance between unrelenting fatigue and overwhelming love. Your soul aches to nurture your child in the best possible way, yet that goal feels out of reach. You are constantly chasing, and never quite achieving. Your brain struggles to focus, making it difficult to sift through the influx of information, advice, encouragement, and support.

It feels like a gut punch when you take your baby to their first pediatrician visit and hear the words, "Your baby isn't gaining enough weight." Your mind swirls with shame and doubt. It is your job to ensure your baby receives enough nutrition to grow and thrive, yet you have already fallen short—just one week into being a new mom. This scenario is common, yet it can often be prevented or resolved with the right support and close guidance from an IBCLC to help preserve the breastfeeding relationship. Establishing a strong milk supply and ensuring the baby receives adequate nutrition to grow appropriately are two of the most critical components for long-term success.

Careful, individualized feeding plans are essential for new moms as they learn to trust their intuition and understand biological newborn behavior and feeding norms. Solid information and support exist, but they can be difficult to find. Our world is changing rapidly in how we search and consume information. We have answers to every question immediately at our fingertips, which can be both a blessing and a curse. You can get great information, but you can also stumble across incorrect or inadequate information that throws you completely off course. This can take a toll physically and mentally.

Information Overload

I write specifically to new moms because I am witnessing a cultural shift that is pushing them to their breaking point. Every day, I work with new moms and families navigating challenges with their babies—whether it be feeding difficulties, fussiness, gassiness, or not sleeping well. Mothers blame themselves and desperately seek help. They arrive exhausted and hopeless, knowing something is not quite right yet struggling to find answers, support, or guidance in uncovering the root of the problem.

Support for new moms is severely lacking. Many are left feeling hopeless, bombarded with societal pressures from every direction. It is heartbreaking to witness and hear their stories as I begin to offer hope and help them piece things together so they can truly enjoy motherhood and thrive alongside their babies. Every day, they are faced with social media pressures to sleep train, follow "eat, play, sleep," force their babies to self-soothe, pump excessively to stockpile milk, and more. Society and culture get in the way of allowing mothers to trust their intuition, feel supported, and simply enjoy motherhood.

New mothers also face societal pressure to lose baby weight quickly, return to work immediately, and get their babies to sleep through the night. Society is pushing babies to do things they aren't biologically ready for—like sleep training—which is not developmentally appropriate. These tactics can be confusing for exhausted parents, as marketing strategies prey on their fatigue and vulnerability. As a result, stress and exhaustion increase, leading to unintended consequences such as low milk supply and slow infant weight gain.

It is biologically normal for newborns to wake overnight to nurse. This pattern protects milk supply, ensures babies receive adequate nutrition, and fosters a secure attachment. The hormone prolactin, responsible for milk production, surges overnight, making nighttime feedings crucial for sustaining supply. Overnight nursing also helps protect against SIDS[9] and helps form secure attachment.

Another example of societal interference is the *eat, play, sleep* approach, which attempts to impose an artificial schedule on babies. I recommend learning and following your own baby's cues instead of strictly adhering to a schedule that was invented and does not follow biological design and development. Breastfeeding is designed perfectly for both baby's and mom's bodies to work together and support one another. Baby needs to be able to nurse when they cue for it instead of waiting because it hasn't been long enough between feedings, or because it is nap time and not feeding time. When culture and society get in the way of biological design, it makes life more difficult and frustrating. New moms are impacted and miss out on enjoying their babies. The obsession of fitting babies into preset molds can lead to anxiety, stress, and despair. This impacts the nurturing bond and can disrupt the family unit.

The Importance of a Support System

Finding a care team that supports and surrounds you is vital as you enter motherhood. While challenges may arise, knowledgeable providers can guide you every step of the way. There is hope, and there is help. Every mama wants the very best for her precious babies, and with the right support, she can achieve that goal.

Next, we will explore helpful education strategies and practical solutions for managing feeding difficulties. My goal is to provide simplified, foundational information to help guide you as you seek advanced, individualized care.

The Comparison Trap

It is difficult to resist falling into comparison culture, envying what other people have: most often people we have never even met. Social media pressures are higher than ever. According to *Exploding Topics*, the average American checks their mobile device 159 times a day. Additionally, *Psychology Today* reports that the average person spends 2 hours and 24 minutes on social media daily, with users projected to spend a collective four trillion hours on social media this year.

Social media platforms allow people to edit their lives, creating an illusion of perfection in every way. This can damage onlookers who are not able to separate reality from illusion. A troubling trend is the targeting of new mothers, making them chase an unattainable ideal of pregnancy, birth, breastfeeding, and motherhood. Many mothers compare their worth to the curated lives of strangers on Instagram, leading to exhaustion and frustration.

Have you heard of the echo chamber effect? Research describes how social media algorithms inundate users with content specifically curated to their interests and situation.[10] For example, if a new mom begins following an influencer who discusses having a baby, all of a sudden, her entire feed is filled with everything on that topic. This can quickly escalate to "doomscrolling," information overload, and worry.

I cannot imagine navigating being a new mom under today's societal pressures and the unrelenting chase for perfection. My husband wisely reminds me, "You might be envious of the vacation a person went on, or their perfectly decorated home, or beautiful yard, but would you want to trade your life for theirs? If you take their vacation, you also need to have their job, kids, struggles, and marriage. Everyone has something hard in their life. No one is perfect."

I love what my pastor says also: "Why do you care what someone thinks about you who didn't die for you? Jesus gave His life for you. What He thinks of you is most important."

Knowing where your identity lies and where your strength and joy originate is the most important. With God on your side, you will not only succeed, but you will also find confidence, joy, and fulfillment in your journey—even when it is difficult (Ps. 139:13–14).

Managing Latching and Feeding Difficulties

Recognizing red flags and confidently knowing how to intervene when things aren't going as planned are key to managing the challenges that arise when your baby is not latching and transferring milk properly. There are many reasons why babies do not nurse optimally after birth. The two most important actions in managing the situation are: first, ensuring baby receives the appropriate volume of milk; and second, ensuring adequate maternal stimulation and milk removal to protect supply and signal to the maternal brain and hormones that lactogenesis is progressing and milk volume needs to increase.

How do we do this? If baby is not feeding well from the breast and they are twenty-four hours old, it is time to intervene. This involves a two-step process: feeding the baby and stimulating and removing milk from the breast. If baby requires supplementation for medical reasons, it is imperative to begin hand-expressing and pumping on a schedule to signal to the body that milk production must continue.

Watch for These Red Flags:

- Baby is unable to achieve a latch and is twenty-four hours old
- Severe nipple trauma including blisters, cracks, bleeding, bruising, or misshapen nipples after baby unlatches
- Excruciating nipple pain that persists through the entire feeding
- Inadequate diaper count
- High percentage weight loss
- Fussiness and inability to be soothed after breastfeeding
- High bilirubin levels or jaundice
- Low blood sugar (especially common with early-term delivery, premature delivery, maternal diabetes, small for gestional age (SGA), or large for gestational age (LGA))
- Early-term birth (37+0 to 38+6 weeks' gestation)
- Late preterm birth (36 to 37 weeks' gestation)
- Preterm birth (prior to 36 weeks' gestation)
- Pediatrician recommends supplemental feedings

Activate the Plan:

- Contact an IBCLC for guidance
- Hand-express prior to each feeding attempt and prior to pumping sessions
- Begin pumping every two to three hours for ten to fifteen minutes (after baby nurses if baby is latching), using a double electric breast pump
- Use correctly sized breast pump flanges (ideally fitted by an IBCLC before delivery)
- Syringe-feed using the finger-feeding method with appropriate volumes
- Continuously assess progress with milk supply, milk transfer while breastfeeding, and baby's weight gain

This list is a good start. It gives you an action plan to follow right away while you seek a skilled provider to help you manage the feeding and pumping plan according to you and your baby's specific needs. The early days are so important in the long-term total milk volume production, so it is vital to know and understand when and how to intervene to protect the breastfeeding relationship. There should be frequent assessments of latch quality, milk transfer efficiency, diaper output and weight gain, and ensuring milk volumes are increasing appropriately when pumping. This is why it is critical to have trusted, skilled providers helping to guide you and update the plan as needed.

Formula supplementation is medically recommended in some cases, but sometimes it is unnecessary and ends up disrupting the intricate design of a breastfeeding relationship between mom and baby. The knowledge in this book will help new mothers avoid common pitfalls that can interfere with successful breastfeeding and have lasting impacts. I want to bring attention to the pitfalls that can occur without guidance on your journey.

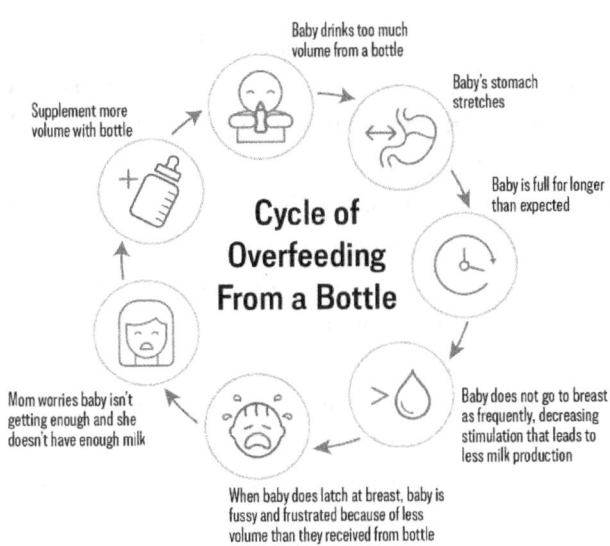

Baby drinks too much volume from a bottle

Baby's stomach stretches

Supplement more volume with bottle

Baby is full for longer than expected

Cycle of Overfeeding From a Bottle

Mom worries baby isn't getting enough and she doesn't have enough milk

Baby does not go to breast as frequently, decreasing stimulation that leads to less milk production

When baby does latch at breast, baby is fussy and frustrated because of less volume than they received from bottle

Supplemental Feeding Techniques

Finger Feeding

Finger feeding is an excellent technique when a baby is not latching to the breast, but requires supplemental milk. I love this technique because it allows the baby to realize that suck and swallow pair together, versus just pushing milk from a syringe straight into the baby's mouth or cheek pocket. With finger feeding, the suck reflex is triggered by gently stimulating the baby's hard palate with your index finger to engage and elicit the suck reflex. Then, you can slowly push colostrum, expressed breast milk, or formula through the syringe as baby is learning and regulating their suck-swallow-breathe pattern. This method allows their reflexes to help with effective feedings in the first few days, and it makes it easier to return to breastfeeding. You will not risk early flow preference or overfeeding volume using this technique as sometimes can happen with bottle-feeding in the early days.

Paced Bottle-Feeding

Paced bottle-feeding is a technique used to control the flow of the bottle so the baby does not drink too quickly or have difficulty managing the flow, which can lead to overfeeding, poor overall quality feeding, reflux, and breast refusal. The correct volume is immensely important in the first few days to provide adequate intake without being overfed and consuming more milk than their mom is making. Colostrum volumes are naturally small, and overfeeding can create an imbalance. More important than just telling parents to hold the baby upright and keep the bottle horizontal is teaching them how to identify a quality feeding. When I teach new parents bottle feeding, I teach them baby's cues, sucking patterns, and body language to help parents pace the feeding appropriately. Careful selection of nipple shape and flow rate are also an important part of the process.

ABM Supplementation Protocol #3

Average Reported Intakes of Colostrum
by Healthy Term Breastfed Infants

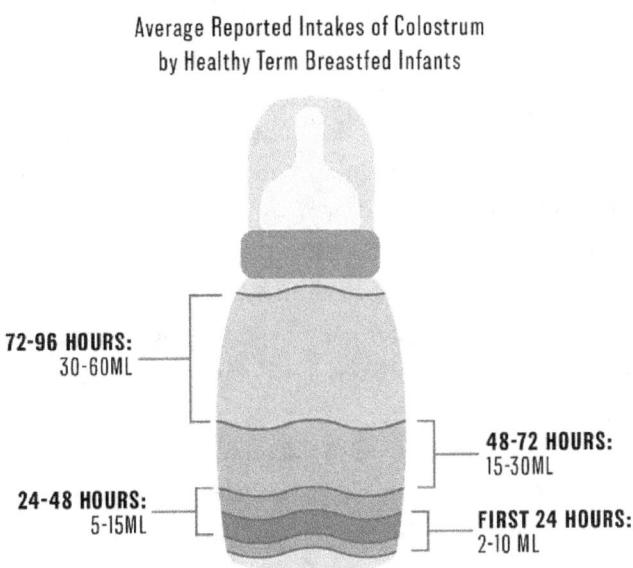

72-96 HOURS:
30-60ML

48-72 HOURS:
15-30ML

24-48 HOURS:
5-15ML

FIRST 24 HOURS:
2-10 ML

Cup Feeding/Spoon Feeding

Cup or spoon feeding is another alternative to provide supplemental feedings for your baby. Use expressed breast milk or formula on a spoon and slowly tip the edge of the spoon allowing the baby to lick or lap up the milk. Cup feeding is similar. Use a special infant cup to slowly tip the edge of the cup so the baby is able to slowly lap the milk. This is an alternative to use if you are wanting to avoid artificial nipples and bottles.

The Importance of Support and Mental Health

Recognizing feeding difficulties and implementing an action plan can help tremendously in maintaining your confidence and protecting the breastfeeding relationship. Understanding the process can decrease your stress and allow you to focus on nurturing and bonding with your baby. Feeding challenges will arise, but we need to remember to focus on feeding the baby and protecting the milk supply. Surrounding yourself with uplifting encouragement and support will ensure a healthy mentality to sustain your current feeding plan. Skilled IBCLCs are vital in providing individualized guidance, feeding plans, and progress assessments.

New mamas, I want you to hear me when I say, you've got this. You are the perfect mom for your baby. Your baby loves and accepts you just as you are, and they don't need any fancy equipment or gadgets. The importance of nurturing secure attachment should be championed. Instead, new moms are shamed or scared into thinking they are going to raise co-dependent babies who will never sleep on their own and will be spoiled by being held or nursed to sleep. However, attachment theory research contradicts this misconception.

John Bowlby and Mary Ainsworth were players in theorizing and developing attachment theory. Through their studies, they concluded that early attachment between newborns and caregivers has a huge impact that continues throughout their lives.[11] Most behaviorists limited attachment to solely meeting nutrition needs. However, Bowlby and other theorists demonstrated caregiver responsiveness and nurturing were primary determining factors for the formation of secure attachment bonds. The nurturing of feeding is just as important to a baby's growth and development as the nourishment.

Alarmingly, one in five mothers experience a perinatal mood and anxiety disorder (PMAD). It is crucial for health professionals to be trained in screening for signs of PMADs and to effectively validate and communicate therapeutically. You are not alone if you are struggling and feeling hopeless. I urge you to contact someone for help and support if you are struggling internally or need help processing. The shift in hormones happening in the immediate postpartum period is the biggest shift in the shortest amount of time our bodies will ever go through. This can be exacerbated by birth trauma or feeding difficulties. Imagine this massive hormonal shift while navigating birth trauma or grief and then having challenges feeding your baby. This can be weighty and difficult to manage on your own. The thoughts can swirl around in your mind like a continuous cyclone, growing bigger and more uncontrollable by the day.

Mental health disorders are at an all-time high due to chronic stress and our modern tendency to live in a state of fight-or-flight. This prolonged stress dysregulates the nervous system, impacting all aspects of life. If you are experiencing stress or anxiety, please reach out for help. Find a trusted support system to navigate these feelings, reinforce your confidence, and restore your joy in motherhood.

Comparison Culture

*Now to Him who is able to do far more abundantly than we
ask or think, according to the power at work within us.*
Ephesians 3:20

THE YELLOW WOODEN rocking chair in the corner of
the nursery was my favorite place to be in our tiny home. The
intricately carved flowers formed an arch across the top of the
chair's frame—those flowers were my favorite part. This one-of-a-kind
chair had so much character. Its pale, yellow cushion was perfectly
soft and comforting. My tired yet grateful body sank into it day after day and night after night as I nursed and rocked my babies well
beyond their initial drifting off to sleep. I didn't want to put them
down—especially after a night spent twelve hours away from them
while at the hospital, helping other mamas welcome their sweet babies
while mine were asleep at home. At home again, I felt calm and happy
holding my babies safe and close while we gently rocked.

There is nothing quite like carefully studying each of your baby's
tiny features and watching them breathe so easily and deeply, so full
of peace. No matter how hectic, stressful, or overwhelming the day

could be, the yellow rocking chair was an envelope of peace for us both. We both knew we were safe. We both knew we were loved. We both knew we could rest.

There were (and still are) many times I second-guessed myself as a mom. I was a night nurse and worked three twelve-hour shifts a week. Three days out of the week, I was not there for my babies if they woke up at night hungry, cold, or scared. Praise the Lord for an incredible husband who loves our kids so much. He is the only reason I was able to leave my babies. I knew without a doubt he would be there for them in a heartbeat. He is the best dad, and our kids are so incredibly blessed to have him. But it didn't take away the feelings I had of self-doubt and heartache from leaving them.

I worked night shifts so I could be with them the most hours possible while also working full time. I sacrificed so much sleep, but they were worth it. I would schedule myself to work every other night because I would miss them too much if I worked two nights in a row. Every night I went to work, I would be awake more than twenty-four hours. I would get up in the morning like normal, have a full day, and then leave for work, already exhausted before my twelve-hour shift even began. Thank goodness I was young and resilient. I did it for my kids, but I still couldn't shake the feeling that I was doing it *to* them. I was choosing to work as a nurse and be away from them.

I had friends who stayed home and were with their babies always. I envied that life and wished it were mine. I often wondered if I was doing the right thing. Would my kids remember? Would they wonder why sometimes I had to sleep during the day? Would they wonder why I was taking care of other babies and not them? The questions swirled in my mind and led me down the road of comparison culture.

Comparison culture is a slippery slope. Once you start the descent, it is hard to change course, especially as you gain speed. Today's culture makes it increasingly difficult, as we can glimpse through our screens into all the perfect angles and details of everyone else's lives.

With each swipe up bombarded with images of seemingly perfect lives. Stuck in our own heads, we get tangled up in lies and darkness, losing sight of the exit and the light.

The Doomscroll

Enter the doomscroll—we've all been there. We pick up our phone far too often, "just to check" social media. Our default is to open an app whenever we have a spare moment: at a stoplight, waiting in the grocery store checkout line, waiting in the car pick up line, waiting for an appointment. We don't want to miss out. The rabbit trail leads us further and further away from ourselves.

We get caught up glimpsing into stranger's lives, where everything seems beautiful and perfect. We are immediately consumed with self-doubt. We question everything. We begin to compare and second-guess our own intuition and mothering capabilities when we see an influencer posting about how she feeds her baby, all the baby gadgets and supplies she has, and how she has stored up one thousand ounces of breastmilk in her freezer. We feel inadequate and deflated.

We live in a consumer society. Technological advancements have made it too easy and instant to consume content at any moment. Comparison culture is real. We fall out of reality quickly, and this impacts us and those around us in countless ways. As a holistic practitioner, I always look to the root of problems, evaluating the layers that impact mind, body, and soul. Our health and well-being suffer when one or all of these pieces are affected.

Moms have it especially hard because not only do we lambaste ourselves individually, but we are also responsible for other little lives. We judge ourselves harshly and regularly berate ourselves about the choices we make in raising our kids. It is so easy to look at other moms—at the nurseries they have so intricately decorated, their beautiful birth stories, their gorgeous photoshoots, and the perfectly planned first birthday parties—and ultimately feel like failures if we cannot measure up in the same outward, earthly ways.

Have you ever had the wind knocked out of your sails when confronted with something you were not doing or hadn't done in motherhood? I know I have! Some examples for me include not having my kids participate in all the sports and activities all the time, not going to the library weekly for story-time, not having a themed nursery or themed birthday parties—or not having birthday parties at all, for that matter! It can feel defeating and embarrassing at times.

I'm here to tell you to ignore the lies that culture and society try to feed you. You are beautiful and perfect, and you are the perfect mom for your babies. Lives, situations, and experiences are all different, but that doesn't make one better than the other. There are resources at the back of this book to help guide you if needed. Social media can be incredibly damaging to women and mothers, as we are constantly reminded of all the things we don't have and aren't doing. We can so easily get discouraged and lose our joy when we are in a tough headspace and then mindlessly open an app that seems to reinforce all our negative thoughts. Please, I beg you, do not use the internet as a gauge for self-worth and success. You are a unique individual designed for a specific purpose in this life. You are worthy of love and created to enjoy life, experience it to the fullest, and have a positive impact on the world around you.

I remember feeling alone as a new mom. There I was, standing in our living room, holding my nine-day-old crying newborn and not knowing how to help her. The adrenaline from birth had worn off, the visitors were gone, my husband was back at work, and there I was, just me and my new baby daughter crying together. Thank goodness for my support system, which helped me immensely in learning how to be a mom.

Breastfeeding is a natural process, but it doesn't always come naturally. It is a learned skill. Newborn care and bottle feeding also do not just come naturally; they, too, are learned skills that require practice and time to optimize feeding and make it the best quality for the baby. Learning your baby's specific cues and tending to their needs with confidence also comes with time. The more time you spend with your baby, the easier this will become.

Newborn babies thrive and grow best with human touch and responsiveness. During their first six months of life outside the uterus, they learn to trust and form secure attachment bonds that will stay with them and benefit them throughout their lifetime. Learning how to calm and soothe your baby and recognizing their cues for hunger, sleepiness, and discomfort will come with time. It can all feel overwhelming and foreign if you have never held or cared for a newborn before. The unknowns and lack of confidence can take their toll on new parents' mental and physical health. I remember all too well the feelings of inadequacy and hopelessness from being unable to soothe my baby. I immediately equated what I didn't know and what I wasn't able to accomplish with my overall worth as a mother. It was a dark and sad place to be. I could have very easily found myself at the bottom of the pit of despair if I had not reached out for help and support. My support system made me feel like a good mom and helped teach me without shaming or judging me.

The quality of feedings directly impacts a baby's comfort, sleep, growth, and development. If these things are impacted for a baby, mom can also be impacted emotionally and physically. You can see how the cycle begins and how it can continue to impact new parents when they don't know where to turn or how to help their baby.

Cultivating Confidence

Something profound happens when we fully grasp God's providence and power. We are able to look beyond ourselves to something greater and relinquish the control we only think we have over our own lives.

God has already written our stories. He knew us before we were born, and He designed us with a specific and unique plan and purpose (Jer. 1:5). Doesn't that make you feel so good? Don't you feel freedom in hearing that? I just spontaneously breathed a huge sigh of relief even as I typed out these words. There is power in speaking the truth. When we fully trust God, equip ourselves with solid knowledge, and lean into motherhood knowing we are not alone, we are able to enjoy raising our babies without allowing the added stressors that our society and culture place on our shoulders to derail us.

Seeking knowledge and wisdom is a critical step in cultivating confidence in whatever situation we may be facing. First and foremost, of course, we should hit our knees and ask the Lord to help us, guide us, and lead us in the way we should go. Then we seek out knowledge and wisdom based in truth. Have you ever been frozen in fear when a big life transition hit, or when you squinted and saw it approaching on the horizon? It can feel paralyzing when your brain gets stuck in that negative feedback loop of all the "what ifs" and, in my mom's words, the "woulda, coulda, shouldas" in life. We lean into the calling and task that God has entrusted to us—to raise the baby He created specifically for us. We trust and rely on Him to stand in the gap and fill in where we fall short. That's when true freedom and joy are found.

Uncertainty, unrealistic expectations, and unexpected outcomes are three of the most common challenges that I see new moms face, and if left unchecked, they can be detrimental to joy and homeostasis in the postpartum period. The postpartum period is something else, let me tell you. Through my experience as a labor and delivery nurse at a very busy hospital with a level III NICU and my work as a private practice lactation consultant, I have encountered countless situations that were less than ideal and often completely unavoidable. I have witnessed the best day of people's lives and the worst day of people's lives during one of the biggest life transitions possible. I have cried countless tears of joy and countless tears of sadness. I have stood in the thick of it with my patients in moments of extreme uncertainty, pain, and doubt. Having support, direction, and a plan of action can pull you out of that place of desperation and renew your hope.

Do the Next Thing

I want you to know that sometimes in life, we do everything right. We prepare in every way possible, we dream and imagine the perfect outcome into a beautiful tapestry in our mind, yet the waters of challenge and difficulty still rise. This is not failure; this is part of life on earth. What matters most is the next move. We pivot, we backpedal, we shift, we sidestep—we persevere and find the way. I love this quote by Elisabeth Elliot that my mom has shared with me: "Sometimes life is so hard you can only do the next thing. Whatever that is, just do the next thing. God will meet you there." We need the confidence and direction to know what to do when the days seem dark, and the nights feel long. There is help—you do not have to face the uncertainty and struggle alone.

Feeling alone is terrifying. It makes it extremely hard to take the first step, any step, in any direction. You want so badly to enjoy your baby, to enjoy motherhood, and to know that your baby is comfortable, happy, and healthy. You don't want to feel stressed or anxious, questioning everything you are doing and how it will impact your baby.

I truly believe we all find happiness and confidence when our identity is rooted in Jesus. He designed us and created us exactly as we were meant to be. We are all living the story He has written for us, and we are all part of His master story. When our worth and identity are found in Him, we are more easily able to trust our own intuition—the intuition He has instilled in us. He designed your body to carry and sustain the life of your sweet baby. He designed it so perfectly and intricately. He loves us so much that He created us as mothers to grow and develop babies from single cells. The processes of pregnancy, childbirth, and breastfeeding are incredible and so perfectly created to work together. The biological design was not by mistake.

The connection we have to our babies helps us to mother and allows both us and our babies to thrive and flourish as we go through life together. They say a mother's love is fierce. It is true. There is no love quite like it. In some ways, it makes me stop and think how Jesus loves us. His love is never failing, and nothing can change it. Likewise, the love a mother has for her child is completely unwavering and stronger than any other. We were all created in His image. When we know Him and walk with Him, we abide in Him, and He encourages us to be the mothers He created us to be. How much joy and freedom are in that?!

Let's break the curse of comparison culture and trust in God to sustain us and lead us. We will continue to fall short when we rely on the things of this world to bring us happiness and fulfillment. When we allow Jesus in—to change our hearts and abide in us—we experience an outpouring and overflowing of fruit that is undeniable. He changes everything, and our lives are forever transformed in Him. When I was finally able to trust God and rely on Him to sustain and guide me in raising my kids, I found freedom. I stopped constantly worrying and comparing myself and my kids to others around us. He continues to show me that He is the ultimate healer, giver, and sustainer of all things. It brings sweet relief to know that He is in control, that He will pick me up when I fall short, and that He is filling the gap when I get it wrong.

I often think back to my breastfeeding journey with my first two babies, and my only regret is not realizing that I could have reached out to a lactation consultant for guidance. My story would have been different if I had known that seeking help was an option. Yet, I am grateful for all my experiences and everything I learned, including what I regret not doing, because they help me to be more empathetic and understanding with the moms I work with. I have been in your shoes. I have been on both sides of the coin. I have experienced doubt, shame, fear, and failure—but also joy, fulfillment, and redemption. That can be your story too.

EPILOGUE

Seeking Support

I DID THE BEST I could with the information I had at the time. I prayed that God would stand in the gap, fix my shortcomings, protect my kids, and help me help them flourish in life. Parenting is hard; life is a journey filled with mountains and valleys. Comparison culture is real. Times have changed and continue to change at an alarming pace. I see firsthand the pressures new moms face daily, and it breaks my heart. I see the distress and worry they shoulder. Society today, heavily influenced by social media, makes it incredibly difficult for new moms to trust their own abilities and innate intuition to raise their babies as they feel led.

If we aren't careful, life will pass us by. We will miss it—or, even scarier, we will not enjoy it. God gives us all one life to live, and it is a gift. He wants us to run the race well (2 Tim. 4:6–8). We must recognize this to fully experience all that life has to offer, both its ups and downs. My husband reminds me how incredible it is to be alive, how life can be so full (in a good way), and how it is meant to be lived and experienced. I have journeyed through many different seasons of motherhood and parenting thus far (and my role as a mom will never actually end). My firstborn daughter is heading into her senior year of high school and my youngest son is preparing to start kindergarten. We are about to have kids in college, high school, middle school, and elementary school all at the same time! Parenting has been one wild ride, shaping me into the woman God has called me to be.

My true passion lies in seeking and encountering God daily, being the wife God called me to be, raising my babies to seek God and have a living relationship with Jesus, honoring God in my business, and supporting new moms as they begin their own unique journeys. My daily question to myself is, *How can I be the hands and feet of Jesus today in this meeting, interaction, phone call, consult, challenge, business decision, or opportunity?* There is so much awe, joy, and wonder in being a parent.

Seeking out and establishing your support team prior to your baby's arrival can make a night-and-day difference in your experience as you transition into motherhood. There is so much to learn, and there are so many moving parts to the process. It can feel isolating and overwhelming very quickly, especially if you wait to ask for help until a challenge or unexpected outcome arises after your baby's arrival. Gaining as much knowledge and understanding as you can ahead of time will help you in moments of stress and despair because you have wisdom to draw from and rely on. It is very difficult to learn something new and implement it once you are in crisis mode.

I cannot stress enough the importance of contacting an IBCLC prenatally to guide you with infant feeding. Feeding difficulties and challenges can wreak havoc on your ability to enjoy your baby stress-free from birth. Many mamas have so much stress from their initial latch and breastfeeding attempt during the golden hour. When feeding is a struggle, you automatically begin worrying about your baby's nutrition, weight gain, growth, and well-being. This, in turn, leads to constant worry and obsessive tracking of feedings, diapers, and sleep. The obsession with tracking and overanalyzing everything takes your attention away from relaxing and enjoying your newborn. Remember, when mama is stressed, babies are not able to co-regulate well. Babies need their mama's body and nervous system to help them regulate their immature nervous system. Finding your support team is crucial in helping you prepare as best as possible before your baby's arrival—and ensuring you have your team available immediately if difficulties arise. You will feel great confidence knowing you have someone who can help assess and guide you with appropriate steps to keep everything on track from the start. Even if the beginning is shaky or unexpected, you will find success and joy.

I cannot tell you how many mamas I have worked with who were grateful for the prenatal education and support they received, which helped them lower stress levels and increase their confidence in successfully beginning breastfeeding. Likewise, I have had many mamas with unexpected outcomes and challenges who were equally grateful to have me in their corner to help guide, support, and encourage them. There is a clear correlation between support, encouragement, guidance, and decreased stress and increased confidence.

I also want to encourage you to have a support system in place for you and your baby in other ways, both before and after birth. When you feel aligned with and supported by your care team, you will enter your birth space with confidence, knowing you have a system in place to call on if needed. It can feel difficult to make decisions and seek out professionals when you are already worried and overwhelmed.

Press into God—pray and ask for guidance and help. Ask Him to give you strength, wisdom, and confidence. Surrender all your worries and let Him bear your burdens daily (Ps. 68:19). Please reach out if you need help finding and connecting with certain providers in your area; I am happy to help. I am also happy to support you virtually if you are outside the Kansas City area.

I am so proud of you and so excited for you. You are a great mom, and you are exactly who your baby needs. You and your baby are designed to thrive.

Acknowledgments

First and foremost, I want to thank God for calling me to write this book and helping me complete it. He placed the idea in my head and encouraged me to put these words on paper. I pray He is glorified in these pages and you are blessed by reading them.

I thank my family for the encouragement, love, and sacrifice in helping me complete this work. To my husband, Joel—I love you. Thank you for believing in me and encouraging me to follow God's prompting on my heart. You stood by my side and never questioned it.

I want to thank my awesome kids for cheering me on and being excited for me as I worked late nights and early mornings to accomplish this.

To my parents, Suzanne and Ron Forsberg—thank you for always listening, praying for me continually, and encouraging me to listen to the Holy Spirit's whisper to complete this book. You have always believed in me with unwavering support. Thank you for investing in my heart and my life and for raising me to be who I am today. I love you both dearly.

To my amazing in-laws, Renee and Tim Gustafson—thank you for your constant prayers and uplifting support. I love you both and am blessed to have you in my life.

A huge thank you to Dr. Jess Bohlke for being a catalyst in encouraging me to launch my business and for cheering me on daily. Your perfectly timed words of wisdom have been honey to my soul.

Thank you to my incredible team at Streamline Books for helping me make this book a reality. Thank you to Traci, my editor—a true Godsend—and to Chloie and Will for believing in my book. Thank you from my whole heart.

About the Author

Lindsay is passionate about helping moms and babes flourish in life. She is a registered nurse and an International Board Certified Lactation Consultant who owns and operates her private practice, Nourish & Flourish, in Overland Park, Kansas.

She has been married for nineteen years and has four awesome kids and a dog. She loves anything involving the outdoors and spends her free time with her family playing sports outside, hiking, playing board games, and training in endurance sports with her husband.

Endnotes

1 Donna Geddes and Sharon Perrella, "Breastfeeding and Human Lactation," Nutrients 11, no. 4 (April 9, 2019): 802. doi:10.3390/nu11040802.

2 Geddes, "Breastfeeding."

3 Geddes, "Breastfeeding and Human Lactation."

4 Camille Le Maître et al., "Feto-Maternal Microchimerism: Memories from Pregnancy," *iScience* 25, no. 1 (January 21, 2022): 103664.

5 Geddes, "Breastfeeding and Human Lactation."

6 Ann-Marie Widström et al., "Skin-to-Skin Contact the First Hour after Birth, Underlying Implications and Clinical Practice," *Acta Paediatrica* 108, no. 7 (July 2019): 1192–1204.

7 Geddes, "Breastfeeding and Human Lactation."

8 Geddes, "Breastfeeding and Human Lactation."

9 Fern R. Hauck, et al. "Breastfeeding and Reduced Risk of Sudden Infant Death Syndrome: A Meta-Analysis," Pediatrics, 128, 1 (2011): 103-10. DOI: 10.1542/peds.2010-3000; Rachel Y. Moon, et al. "Sleep-Related Infant Deaths: Updated 2022 Recommendations for Reducing Infant Deaths in the Sleep Environment," Pediatrics, 150, 1 (2022): e2022057990. https://doi.org/10.1542/peds.2022-057990.

10 Gao, Yichang et al. "Echo Chamber Effects on Short Video Platforms." Scientific Reports vol. 13,1 6282. April 18. 2023, doi:10.1038/s41598-023-33370-1

11 John Bowlby, Attachment and Loss: Vol. I: Attachment. (New York: Basic Books, 1969); and Mary Ainsworth, et al. Patterns of Attachment: A Psychological Study of the Strange Situation (Hillsdale, NJ: Erlbaum, 1978).